CHRISTOPHER KNIGHT'S

St. Helena:

"HEARTSTOPPING!! ONE WILD RIDE OF ALL-OUT TERROR!"
-Gerry Franzen, WRBZ, Raleigh-Durham

"IMAGINATIVE AND SUSPENSEFUL!
-Katie Riccio, WMGN,WTDY, Madison

"A MASTERFUL WORK OF TERROR."
-Clay Carson, KRBE, Houston

"A TRULY TERRIFYING TALE!"
-Ross Boissineau, Traverse City Record-Eagle

"A FIRST-RATE TOP NOTCH THRILLER!!"
-Tom Elliot, Critics' Review Magazine

"MICHIGAN'S NEW MASTER OF THE MACABRE."
-Dave Roberts, Columbia Audio, Rockford

"A SPECTACULAR STORY OF THRILLING SUSPENSE."
-Tony King, KKPN, Houston

"SUSPENSE TIMES TEN!"
-Chuck Mefford, Mefford Achievement Systems, Dallas

Other books by Christopher Knight:

St. Helena

Ferocity

The Laurentian Channel

Christopher Knight

St.

Helena

This book contains the complete
unabridged text of the original work.
It has been set in a typeface
designed for easy reading and
was printed from new film.

ST. HELENA

An AudioCraft Publishing, Inc. book

ISBN: 1-893699-00-5

AudioCraft Books are published by
AudioCraft Publishing, Inc., PO Box 281, Topinabee Island, MI 49791

Printed in the United States of America

The author wishes to thank Dick Moehl for his invaluable information and resources; Chuck Beard and Straits Area Printing for 'above and beyond'; Dave McCauslin of DM Consulting for taming the Computer Beast; Maureen MacLaughlin for sharing her knowledge; and- Captain Eric Berkey for the wild ride.

Dear Reader:

The Great Lakes will always remain a mystery to me. Stories of days long ago continue to permeate history; stories of ships and shipwrecks, ghost towns, and... *Lighthouses*.

St. Helena (pronounced hel-LEEN...the 'a' is silent) is one such island that has drawn my particular fascination. The story initially had been in my head for over a year, and while driving across the Mackinac Bridge one evening I caught a glimpse of the St. Helena Island lighthouse in the distance. Abandoned for years and very desolate, the island seemed like a perfect setting for some type of macabre thriller...thus, St. Helena Island and its lighthouse became the 'adopted' harbor for my imagination...at least in this particular story. As ideas churned, I wondered what it would be like to write the story as an 'audio book'...or book-on-tape as some prefer. Not just a narrator reading a story, but a full theatrical presentation complete with music and sound effects. The resulting abridged work took well over 600 hours of narration, production, mixing and mastering, packed into a 3-hour story on two cassettes. However, had I attempted to produce the audio book as 'unabridged' (as it is offered to you in the work you are holding) I'm certain the project would still be in production, not to mention far over budget. Music royalties and other expenses can be astronomical; hence the only real way to make the 'complete version' of St. Helena affordable would be to offer it in trade paperback, as you now have in your hands.

And another note:

Although St. Helena Island is very real, the story, (as my publisher has stated earlier in these pages) is that of fiction. The characters, people, etc. within these pages simply do not exist. There are, however, many geographical and historical facts woven within the story that are entirely true...others are simply a wild fabrication of my own. Perhaps that's what fascinates me most about this occupation: authors have free editorial license to use the truth however we see fit, should we decide to use it at all.

What is real and what is not has been left for the reader to decide.

Christopher Knight
November 21, 1998

And for all this, die will he not;
There is no man sees him but I;
You came and went and forgot;
I hope he will some day die.

-Algernon Charles Swinburne, 1868

....Sorry 'bout yer luck.

-Tom Pearson, 1998

PROLOGUE

July, 1883

Ten-year old Virgil McClure ran furiously, racing along the thin, winding path that snarled and twisted through the thick cedar swamp. His footsteps drummed the narrow trail and his parched lungs ached, screaming for breath. Sharp tree branches snapped and tore at the tender flesh of his young face and a trickle of blood ran down the side of his cheek where a limb had struck, creating a dirty maroon river that coiled over his jawbone and branched down his neck.

neck. His forehead glistened with sweat and a line of perspiration stained the back of his shirt, snaking along his backbone and creating a thin wet smudge that began at his collar and stretched all the way to his trousers. Virgil could hear the other boys not far behind him, laughing and taunting, howling with bloodthirsty excitement. Their eager shouts and chants echoed through the forest, and with each piercing wail Virgil's terror grew. Cedar trees flew by as he ran frantically through the thick underbrush of the island. His mind was a blur as his thin legs pumped harder and harder, pushing himself desperately to go faster and faster or else once again suffer the inevitable consequences. Virgil snapped his head around just for an instant and shot a panicked glance behind him. He was unable to see the boys through the dense foliage, but their wild, excited shrieks had grown louder. They continued to gain on him, but he thought if he could keep up this pace for just a little longer he could out-distance his assailants and make it to the safety of his home in time to get inside. His father would still be gone on errands and his mother...well, his mother would *always* be gone. She had died a few years back while giving birth to Virgil's brother. And when *he* had died, only young Virgil and his father had been left to tend the lighthouse on the island of St. Helena. The bright beacon was a welcome sight to ships that traveled the dangerous Straits of Mackinac. The light was a guide, a reassurance to sailors as they made their way through the shoal-filled waters. To captains and crews, the St. Helena lighthouse was a comforting sight indeed.

But for Virgil McClure, it was much more than just a

lighthouse.

It was *home*.

His feet pounded the soft ground and he snapped his head around again, just in time to catch quick flashes of clothing through the trees. The group of boys numbered at least six, probably more.

In the next moment Virgil found himself on the ground in a whirl of dust and sand, tumbling over the hard packed surface of the trail. He had fallen. Ignoring the pain of two scraped knees, Virgil bounded up and began to run again with a determination brought upon by fear and dread.

Why?!?!? he thought, as he stretched his legs further. *Why do they do this to me?!?!* For as long as he could remember, the other children on the island mocked him and teased him, and he had seen more than one fight in his short ten years. He dreaded having to go to the tiny school on the island. Often he was forced to run most of the way home to escape the punishing beatings by the local bullies. A few weeks ago some boys had cornered him on the outskirts of the village, chanting and calling him names, spitting on him, pushing him around in the tight circle. They had swarmed like angry bees, taking turns kicking and hitting him, knocking him to the ground. When the melee was spotted by an alert adult the boys had fled, but not before Virgil sustained a bloody nose and a gash over his right eye. And there had been many other such incidences as well. Once a few bullies had held him to the ground while others kicked at his stomach and ribs. Again, they probably would have continued were it not for the fact that the schoolteacher had seen them and came to Virgil's rescue.

Of course, there were obvious reasons that Virgil McClure was despised and disliked so much. He was a loner. Virgil didn't play with the other children on the island and was quiet and shy at school. He only spoke to others when he was spoken to, much rather preferring to be left alone. He was *different*...or at least *he* believed he was. And now others had good reason to believe as well.

He continued racing along the turning, twisting path, nearing the forest line where the trees would fall away and a large, lush meadow opened up. Just a few more turns....

"Scaredy Cat!" he heard one of the boys yell from somewhere not far behind him.

"We're going to get you!" screamed another.

"Hey Virgy-Wirgy...where's your brother?? How come your little brother's not going to help ya?!??!" one of them shrieked.

"CAUSE HE'S IN THE GROUND, THAT'S WHY!!" one of the boys answered, his voice howling through the forest. *"HE'S IN THE GROUND, VIRGIL!! HE'S IN THE GROUND AND HE'S NOT EVER COMING OUT!!"* The comment drew a fit of enthusiastic laughter from the other boys as they continued their relentless pursuit.

The conical tower suddenly appeared in the distance, towering gray and white through the tall brush on the other side of the meadow. It spiraled up majestically, high into the afternoon sky, creating a long dark shadow that fell over the field. The adjacent lighthouse, glimmering brightly in the sun with a new coat of white paint, sat somber and quiet next to the soaring tower.

I'm almost home. Almost.

But he would still have to make it across the field.

Virgil managed another quick, panic-stricken glance behind him as he sprinted faster over the thin trail that wove through the bright green knee-high grass. It was thick and long, so long that the leafy tongues grew up and bent sluggishly over the trail, in some places totally obscuring the path.

When Virgil was half way through the field the boys exploded from the forest behind him like savages, their shouts and taunts ringing across the field and echoing over the meadow before dying away at the dense wall of the surrounding forest. Blades of tall grass lashed at Virgil's heels and licked at his trousers like thin paper knives. He tried to run faster still, trying to put more distance between himself and the threatening gang of youths.

He cleared the field and bounded wildly across the porch of the house, his eyes keenly focused on the front door. Wooden boards drummed beneath his feet as he sprang madly towards the parlor door, his arms outstretched long before he reached it. The other boys were so close he could almost feel their hot breath on the nape of his neck like wolves standing over their dying prey, eyeing their helpless victim only moments before tearing ravenously into its soft flesh. He dared not turn around, dared not look back for fear of stumbling again, of falling headlong and not being able to get up.

In a frenzy Virgil twisted at the brass knob and the door burst open. He dashed inside, sneaking a quick glance back to see that the boys had already reached the porch, their mouths wide open in seething mockery. They were smiling and grinning like rabid hyenas, intoxicated by their own cunning deviousness. Virgil slammed the door shut behind him and secured the deadbolt.

Suddenly the door began to shudder and shake as the boys reached it, pounding and slamming their fists into the hard wood. They began beating and slapping at the door, then the side of the house and around to the windows. The noise and shouts reached a fever pitch as the boys ran around the outside of the house, hammering the walls with their palms and shrieking out hostile threats at the very top of their lungs. Virgil quickly ducked behind a cabinet and peered cautiously around the corner, every so often catching a glimpse of a shadow through a window. The pounding at the door and the walls and windows continued for what seemed like forever. Virgil ran upstairs to the secluded safety of his bedroom.

"Si-ssy! Si-ssy! Virgil is a si-ssy!" the boys chanted from the field below. They began running around the house like fiendish animals, banging the walls and pounding at the windows.

"Come on out Virgil!" one of them hollered. *"Come on out ya weirdo...or we'll hafta come in and GITCHA!!"* Their haunting, insolent laughter grew louder and the pounding became more intense. Virgil cringed as their wicked antics reverberated over the meadow below. He inched his way along the wall of his upstairs bedroom and stretched his neck out as far as he could, peering out the window. The boys were still running around the house, pounding and squealing, laughing and jeering. Two of them had taken to throwing rocks, and Virgil could hear the

thuds of stones as they slammed into the side of the lighthouse.

"Whassa matter, Virgil? Is your Daddy gone? Are ya all alone?" One of the boys looked up and smirked as he saw Virgil staring down at them through the second floor window. He pointed upwards then ran to the parlor door, out of Virgil's sight. Another boy looked up at the window where Virgil stood, then he too disappeared as he sprang towards the house.

Virgil heard loud pounding downstairs. A few of the boys were kicking and banging at the front door, and Virgil's whole body shook as he heard the strained lock finally give out. Wood splintered as the bolt broke away, and the heavy wood door creaked slowly open. Virgil crawled beneath the bed, terrified.

They can't come inside! he thought, panicking. *This is my house!! They can't come inside!*

Downstairs in the parlor, the boys drew suspiciously silent. Virgil could hear his heart hammering madly in his chest as he lay on his stomach underneath the bed, his head turned to the side to keep watch over the bedroom door. He heard quiet whispering and snickering coming from downstairs, and the light shuffling of shoes scuffing softly on the wood floor. The stairs began to creak and moan and Virgil cringed, trying to slide closer to the wall and further under the bed.

"Virgil," he heard one of the boys smirk. There was mischief in his voice, an arrogant, brazen tone that reeked of delinquence and disobedience. *"We're coming to gitcha, Virgil,"* the voice mocked. *"We're coming to GITCHA...."*

Virgil could hear more snickering as the boys slowly climbed the steps.

"Come out, come out wherever you are...."

Virgil lay beneath the bed, frozen to the floor. There was nowhere else for him to go, no place to run, no other place to hide. His luck had run out. He was trapped.

And suddenly he remembered a time last summer when he had cornered a young barn cat in the shed. He had watched the animal slink across the yard and through the open door and he quietly crept up on the shed, darting inside and slamming the door closed. It was dark in the cramped storage building except for a few thin holes near the tin roof, enough to let in just a crack of the sun's bright rays. The air was stale and damp, filling Virgil's nostrils and lungs as his eyes adjusted to the darkness. He strained to see the small animal confined in the cluttered shed. With nowhere else to go the kitten had backed itself into a corner, its tiny body shaking with fear. He could see the glossy eyes of the kitten as it stared back at Virgil, two tiny white pin heads within black marbles staring back at him in fright, wondering and waiting. When Virgil slowly reached for the kitten it hissed menacingly, striking out defiantly with its paw. After a few seconds Virgil had finally opened up the door of the shed and allowed the kitten to leave on its own accord, unharmed. He was embarrassed that he had caused so much strife to the poor creature for no more reason than to satisfy the normal curiosity of a young boy. Now, as he lay trapped beneath a metal frame bed in a small room, Virgil realized how the cat must have felt, curled up in a helpless little ball and convulsing in terror, unable to defend itself.

The footsteps reached the top of the stairs. Virgil saw a pair of black shoes appear in the doorway, and then another. Then two more pairs. The boys stood there for the longest time, frozen, making no sound except for the labored whooshing of forced air as each of the boys struggled to catch their breath. The uneasy stillness became a demon, slinking and slithering around the bedroom like a shadow, unseen and unheard. A tiny spider trickled down a fine thread and crawled on Virgil's face, but he was much too terrified to move to swat it. The small creature climbed slowly along the bridge of his nose and over his forehead before scurrying to the floor and crawling away. Virgil had hardly even noticed it. The seconds ticked by, and his heart continued to throb heavily against the wood floor.

"Oh Virgil...." came one if the voices from the upstairs hall. "We know you're up here, Virgil...." The voice was a high-pitched, sing-song taunt, spoken slowly as if to add more drama and effect. None was needed, as Virgil was already paralyzed with fright.

Maybe they don't know where I am, he thought. *Maybe they can't see me. Maybe—*

"Oh Vuuuurjuuull," one of the boys sneered devilishly. *"Come out from under the bed, Virgil...."*

An upside down face appeared as one of the boys bent over to peer under the steel frame bed. A mischievous, wicked grin glared at Virgil, then another, and another. The boys started laughing, their faces contorted in twisted malevolence.

"Hey Virg...you look like you could use a hand!! Come

on, fellas!" One of the boys climbed under the foot of the bed.

"Go away!" Virgil cried. *"Leave me alone!"* He tried to crawl further up into the corner, kicking at the intruder that was trying to grab his skinny, cane-like legs. The boy winced in pain and recoiled as a swift foot from Virgil caught him in the face.

"Owww!! he screamed, recoiling back from the bed and cupping his face with both hands. *"Oh, you're in for it now, Virgil! You're gonna get it now!"* Another boy had climbed under the bed, and together the group began to drag Virgil from beneath it. Virgil was kicking madly, but now the other boys grabbed his legs and pulled him to the center of the room.

The boy that had been kicked cupped his palms around his nose. Blood poured from his nostrils and through his fingers, and a crimson candy-stripe stained his wrists. He lowered his hands and blood continued to run over his lips and down his chin, dripping on to the floor.

Virgil, terrified, lay on his back looking up at the group, waiting for the beating that would surely come. The other boys stood around him in a circle, some looking down at Virgil, others looking at the boy with the bloody nose. Dark red blood continued to flow from his nose and drip from his chin, but the expression of the boy's face had changed. At first he had appeared angry and ready to explode in a fit of rage, but now he was staring at the floor, his face displaying a strange, puzzled look. The other boys took notice and they too followed his gaze to the oak planks beneath their feet.

The blood that was dripping from the boy's chin was disappearing the moment it touched the wood. A large drop ran over his lips and down his chin, the way ice cream drips down the sides of a cone on a hot July afternoon. The thick drop fell from his face and was instantly soaked up by the smooth wood, leaving not even the trace of a stain. Another drip followed and did the same, as if it had fallen down a well, gone forever. The wood floor remained unblemished and unmarked. Virgil watched curiously as the boy, his face bloodied, bent down to look closer at the floor. The boy reached up and dragged his index finger beneath his nose and a droplet of blood remained on the tip of his finger. Slowly, he lowered his hand to the floor. His finger was only inches from the wood and he reached down cautiously, slowly, like he was extending his hand to a dog that he wasn't quite sure was friendly or not. The room was completely still and silent as the other boys looked on. Not a single word was spoken, not a solitary breath was drawn.

The droplet of blood met the wood.

An eerie, low rumble began to growl from deep within the house. The room began to shake, and a picture hanging on a wall crashed to the floor. Virgil, his mouth wide, scooted back from the boy and the rest of the group did the same. An ear-splitting tear ripped through the house, and the boy with the bloody nose began to scream.

"Help me! I can't get...help me! HELP ME!" The other boys watched, horrified, their faces twisted in expressions of shock and disbelief. The boy was being pulled further into the floor, into a gaping black crevice that began widening by the second. A fissure had suddenly

opened up in the floor and the boy tumbled forward, grasping at broken pieces of wood to keep from slipping away into the endless dark dungeon beneath him. His body dangled over the deepening abyss, suspended over black nothingness. A piece of the floor gave in and the plank hurled down into the depths, falling into the vast expanse of darkness below. It was as if the floor had opened up to expose a cave, a never ending hole that sunk to the very core of the earth. The house continued rumbling and shaking, pulling the boy further and further within. Glass could be heard snapping and breaking throughout the house, and it seemed that at any minute the walls and roof would come crashing down. The group of boys stood frozen, their heads snapping around, their eyes wide in disbelief. The quaking shook the floor beneath their feet and the trembling rattled the walls and windows. Below them the hole continued to expand, and the boy struggled harder and harder to break free from the floor that was quickly pulling him within. One arm reached up, grasping at anything, pleading for something firm to clasp.

"Help me!!" He screamed again. *"Please...grab my hand...help me!! HELP ME!!!"* His eyes were wide and filled with horror and he opened his mouth to scream again, but this time he had no chance. It was to be the last time he would ever open his mouth again, the last time he would ever take a breath. With one giant heave that was felt throughout the entire lighthouse the floor seemed to recoil, gaining in strength as it pulled at its helpless victim. A piece of wood that the boy had been clinging to suddenly snapped, and in the next instant he was tumbling

downward, falling in to the deep crevice. He flailed about madly as he plummeted into the darkness, his mouth gaping and his eyes huge and pleading as he disappeared into the black fissure. In seconds the boy was gone and floorboards suddenly began to snap and crack back into place, and broken pieces of wood creaked and moaned as they pulled themselves back together. A moment later the hole was gone and the floor looked again as it had always been.

The house continued to shake and rock and the other boys began screaming as a horrible nightmare came alive before their eyes. They had been too horrified to move, frozen with fear and disbelief, but now they sprang for the door and dashed wildly down the stairs. The house began to shake even more violently and the steel bed frame began to bounce and quake, slamming into the wall. Virgil, too afraid to move, lay on the floor. His eyes were the size of peaches as he gazed at the bed as it twisted and rattled about. Another picture fell from the wall and exploded on the floor. The roar of the house was deafening, and Virgil held his hands tightly over his ears as the shaking grew louder still. Above the noise he could hear the horrified shouts and screams as the other boys fled the macabre scene.

Suddenly, the screaming changed. Shrieks of disbelief and terror became bitter pathetic squeals of pain. It was an excruciating, tormented sound, and shrill anguished cries and pitiful pleas for mercy filled the lighthouse. The screams were inhuman, high-pitched whines that reminded Virgil of the dying wails of a mortally wounded rabbit. He had often hunted with his father and occasionally a rabbit may have only been grazed by the gunshot. The doomed animal would leap erratically through the air, screaming an intense, deplorable shriek that made you want to do anything...*anything*...to make it stop. It was maddening, but thankfully it was Virgil's father who usually grabbed the rabbit by the hind legs and swung the animal head first into the closest tree. Not a laudable way to achieve a death, but then again it was quite effective nonetheless.

Virgil was still frozen to the floor and now he heard the sounds of doors and windows slamming shut. Desperate pounding filled the house, and the frantic wailing became even more intense. The boys were completely trapped. They were screaming and squealing, running from room to room, pounding on walls and windows and doors, searching desperately for an escape. Virgil winced as one of the agonized screeches was cut short, as if sliced in mid-air by some unseen knife. It was as if the lighthouse had come alive, imprisoning the helpless boys within. Only a few minutes had passed since they had dragged him out from beneath the bed, but to Virgil it seemed like hours. His mind was reeling, spinning in clouds of confusion and dread.

One last tormented, agonizing howl thundered through the house, echoing through rooms and filling the air. Virgil heard a loud snap like the sound of a pressure crack ripping through ice on a winter pond, and the torturous wailing of the boy stopped instantly. The turbulent rumbling began to subside and soon the shaking ceased altogether. The St. Helena lighthouse was silent once again.

Virgil lay trembling on the floor for a long, long time.

Finally, after what seemed like hours, he slowly got to his feet, carefully tip-toeing to his bedroom door. Still shaking, he stood in the doorway, listening and watching. His heart leapt madly within his chest, and his shirt echoed every *thump-thump* by shaking ever so slightly. A scraping noise made him jump and he turned, opening his mouth in disbelief. His eyes grew larger still and he took a shaky step backwards.

The picture that had fallen was slowly inching itself back up the wall. Tiny fragments of glass that had broken from the frame now scurried back to the picture. The brittle pieces of glass scraped along the floor like little mice running for the safety of their nest. Virgil was terrified... much more terrified than he had been when the boys were chasing him. But he couldn't move. He just stood there, eyes wide, his mouth gaping, watching the picture as it went about the business of repairing itself. When the glass had been completely restored within the frame the picture slithered across the floor and up the wall to its perch, which was a button-size nail that was about eye level with the boy. The picture stopped, adjusted itself horizontally, and ceased further movement. Virgil's horrified gaze never left the picture as he backed nervously into the upstairs hallway. The photograph had moved under its own power, under its own free will, wandering nonchalantly back to its place as if it were taking its time and had not a care in the world.

A noise came from downstairs. Fear continued to gnaw at him, but somehow there was comfort in that same fear. Oh, he was still quite horrified...yet a strange feeling came over him. He was still very afraid, but somehow he just *knew* that he was not going to be hurt. He just *knew* it. Virgil knew that somehow this bizarre chain of events posed no threat to him. It was a feeling of safety, a feeling of security, like being held tightly in his mother's arms. But that, of course, was no longer possible. His mother's arms were now just a memory, a memory that was fading quickly as he grew older. If it weren't for a few tattered pictures Virgil probably wouldn't remember what his mother had looked like at all.

He crept slowly down the stairs, one cautious step at a time, listening, watching, listening....

At the bottom of the staircase, a large pool of blood was simply *evaporating.* He could see the dark red puddle shrinking, dissipating within the wood floor. The thick liquid seeped into unseen cracks and crevices, disappearing through the floorboards. It was draining somewhere, being sucked away by some hidden pipe or canal. By the time Virgil reached the bottom step the blood was gone, leaving not a hint of its presence. Virgil stared at the wood floor for a long time, straining his eyes, looking for any trace of blood whatsoever. He found none.

The blood had vanished.

Virgil looked around. The parlor was a disaster and in complete shambles. Pictures had been shaken from the walls and lay jumbled about on the floor, their frames breaking from the fall. Furniture was tipped over, a ceramic coffee mug lay in pieces beneath a sideways table...even a few floorboards had snapped in two, unable to withstand the tumultuous quaking. Plaster had fallen from the ceiling and white, chalky dust lay in scattered piles throughout the room. A gentle breeze drifted through a broken window, licking playfully at the torn drape. Virgil stared, his mouth wide open.

A floorboard moved. The motion was very slight, but he caught the subtle movement out of the corner of his eye. Virgil turned his head in the direction of the sound, watching intently.

Outside, a cloud rolled over the sun and an ominous, dark cast fell over the field and forest. Shadows grew darker still, as if night had fallen suddenly and prematurely over St. Helena. The murky gloom enveloped the tiny island, and Virgil could no longer even make out the sparse trees or shrubs that surrounded the lighthouse.

Once again the house began to shudder and shake, only very gently this time. Virgil watched, his ten-year old mind shocked as pieces of glass snapped up from the floor and floated back to their exact positions in the windows. Shards of glass crunched and scraped and cried out as they rushed through the air and returned to their panes, completely restored without as much as a seam in the once again perfect window. The violent shaking and rocking of earlier had caused the house to nearly fall in on itself, but within minutes broken pieces of wood were mending themselves. Tables that had drifted from their places during the quake were now screeching back to position. Virgil caught the flash of a plank that flew up past a window on the outside. All around him the haunting construction work continued. Inside and outside, unseen hands continued to restore the structure. It was as if hundreds of invisible carpenters had gone to work, hastily utilizing their skills to complete the task of reconstructing the entire lighthouse. The low rumbling and the bizarre ghostly repair work continued for nearly a minute while Virgil looked on.

Then, as quickly as it had begun, the quaking stopped. A few short creaks were heard and the penetrating darkness outside began to fade, giving way to an eerie, steely-gray dusk.

And then....

Silence. The air was filled with the deafening roar of- *Nothing.*

The stillness screamed at the island with a haunting loneliness. The tall grass of the meadow, each blade frozen and unmoving, rose up beneath motionless, petrified trees. Enormous evergreens poised immobilized at the edge of the field, their branches hanging sullen and lifeless, their sharp green needles completely still as the silence howled over the island. Even the heavy charcoal sky suspended high above seemed frozen in time, bored and stagnant beneath the distant heavens. It was as if the view outside the window were a photograph, a perfect still-shot like a framed portrait or postcard. There were no buzzing cicadas in the trees, no playful seagulls wheeling and screeching overhead. Tiny sparrows that normally danced and flitted among the young alders were nowhere to be found. Even the calm, lazy gurgle of Lake Michigan only a few dozen yards away was strangely quiet.

But the boys.

Virgil looked around the parlor and strained his neck to look in other rooms, expecting to see a grotesque pile of dead boys, their faces contorted in final expressions of incredible pain and shock. He was sure that they couldn't have escaped, that there was no way possible. He had heard too much, seen too much. There was too much bloodshed, too much catastrophe and mayhem for anyone to make it out alive.

He looked down the hall and through the doorway of the summer kitchen.

Nothing.

Over by the pantry and in the foyer-

Not there.

The boys were gone.

Then, as oddly as the silence had swept over the island, it began to slowly drift away, as a ship goes off to sea quietly in the night. A chickadee suddenly lighted on a branch outside the window, its head cocking quickly to and fro. The small bird flew to the window and lit on the pane, peering in curiously through the thin glass. It remained there for a brief moment, looking through the window, turning its head back towards the woods, then back to the window again. Apparently satisfied, the tiny chickadee flickered off and was gone. The sky began to grow lighter and a single locust started buzzing a soft, monotone drone that grew louder and louder, filling the field and the surrounding trees. Other cicadas began to join in as the sky continued to brighten, and shadows appeared as the sun slowly weaved between giant billowing clouds. Tall blades of grass, olive and tarnished under the overcast sky, were returning to their lush, bright green hue as the sun continued to trickle out in brilliant, piercing beams. A turning his head as the scene outside went through its extraordinary metamorphosis. It was as if he were witness to a re-birth, a re-awakening of sorts. The field and forest had never seemed so vibrantly alive before, teeming with beauty and life and all the wonder it held.

He still hadn't moved from his position at the foot of the stairs and now he took a guarded step forward. His leg was heavy and he felt clumsy, like his limb had gone to sleep from being in the same position for too long. He took another step, stopping when he heard the noise in front of him.

The front door, its bolt now repaired and the molding completely mended, squeaked slowly ajar. There was no breeze to open it, no one standing there with their hand on the knob. It just...*opened.* The heavy door swung steadily open before him, exposing the gleaming green grass of the meadow and the lush emerald branches of the distant cedars on the other side of the field. Finally when the door was wide open it squeaked to a stop, and ten-year old Virgil McClure strode calmly outside and into the bright afternoon sun.

CHAPTER ONE

May, 1998

Ron and Janet Borders stood in the afternoon sun, squinting up at the ominous, run-down structure that was to be their home for the next few years. Two days of growth darkened Ron's jaw, his cheek, his chin, and a portion of his neck. A film of perspiration created a small bead that began to trickle down his forehead and he nodded and wiped away the droplet with the back of his hand, returning his gaze once again to the structure. One hand remained tucked

tucked snugly in the front pocket of his jeans, and his other arm fell to his side as his head slowly turned, appraising the decrepit foundations of the old lighthouse and the poor condition of the conical tower. Although he and his wife had visited the island of St. Helena only a few weeks previous, it seemed that the structure had aged years, if not centuries, in just that short period of time. The lighthouse appeared obviously as Ron had remembered it, but now the cold, haunting loneliness of the deteriorating building seemed more overwhelming than it had on their initial visit. The dingy smell of age filled the air even in the bright sunlight, and the atmosphere was thick and musty like a cold, dark basement. And *lonely.* Ron couldn't help but think that what had happened to the lighthouse had been a terrible tragedy, suffering years upon years of disregard, heaping on season after season of neglect.

Sure is one shitload of work to do, he thought, raising his hand to his forehead to shade his eyes from the glare of the sun.

Somewhere, not far off through a thick line of cedars and aspens, the delighted, unintelligible laughter of children floated through the breeze. Casey, age six, and Jon, age eight, were playing at the shoreline of Lake Michigan, teasing the waves by running after them as the waters drifted back, then howling in amusement as they leapt away when the small waves rushed again to the shoreline. Their excited yelps filtered through the abundant tree branches, and every so often Ron or his wife would glance over through the trees and catch a flash of an orange vest. The children hated wearing the life preservers and had protested loudly, but after a brief minute or two near the lake they completely forgot about the clumsy, buoyant sponge that shrouded their shoulders and strapped around their tiny waists.

Ron smiled as he turned and slipped an arm around his wife. A soft breeze licked at her sandy brown hair and she brushed a lock away from her face that had been swished about by the light wind, and she made another mental note that she needed a trim. Janet had made four or five of the same mental notes over the past two weeks, but with everything going on...the move to St. Helena, storing their belongings on the mainland, outfitting the children with clothing, writing umpteen-dozen various letters to friends and relatives to let them know where she'd be and why she wouldn't be able to call...a visit to the salon just hadn't been on the list of top priorities.

The sun shined brightly over the trees and burned at her eyes, but it felt gloriously warm on her face and arms. Janet loved the sun and spent much time out of doors at the beach or just in the backyard, defiantly disregarding the surgeon general's warnings. Once in a while...once in a *great* while...she would reluctantly smear on some type of sun block if she was going to be in the sun for a long period of time. But even then it wasn't very often. She enjoyed the light tingling and tightness of her skin after a day in the sun...although she tried not to overdo it *too* much. Ultraviolet rays didn't do much to reverse the aging process, and Janet knew that one of these days...probably sooner than later...the ol' age thing would begin creeping in like a snake, slithering upon her silently and without warning, showing its ugly head through the tiny, razor thin wrinkles that had already sprouted on the outskirts of each of her blue eyes. *Roots,* she thought. *That's what they look like. The roots of a tree.* Soon the fine limbs would grow longer and longer, fingering out, reaching toward her temples...and there wasn't a skin cream or miracle potion on the planet that would stop them, no matter what the ads on television said. A little extra sun for the price paid, Janet thought, was well worth it. In the upper Midwest you could count on three months of good summer weather...four if you were really lucky. And in Michigan, if you were fortunate enough to enjoy four *full* months of glorious, delicious summer, you'd better be going to church every Sunday, saying your *Hail Marys* and counting your blessings. The summer months of June, July, and August could be marvelously hot and beautiful in Michigan, but by late September winter loomed in the shadows and her presence could be felt in the cooler air and the brightly colored leaves of the trees as they changed from summer green to purple, orange, red, and all shades in between. Not long after that the brilliant pastel-colored leaves would curl and brown and be torn from their branches by the bitter north winds that howled maliciously from the depths of Canada and the northern plains of the Midwest.

Winter can be so damned long, she often thought when the February ice and snow storms lumbered through. The storms that blew across the Great Lakes could dump two feet of snow or more, easily paralyzing the region. Last year Janet had watched television news coverage of Sault Sainte Marie that showed snow drifted up and over entire houses. The National Guard had been called in to dig people out of their homes and a number of folks had died while stranded in their cars. For sure, Michigan winters could be relentlessly long and cold and tiring. But the welcome arrival of springtime (occasionally in March, usually in April, sometimes not till May) made the colder winter months worth standing. During her first year of college she had spent a winter and the following spring in Maine. She'd heard over and over again about the gorgeous cliffs, the incredible sunrises, the *perfect* eastern summers. But they were no match for the stunning extravagance of Michigan's beautiful rolling hills and playful streams, all coming alive after a long winter of hibernation. The sweets were sweeter, the brights were brighter, and now as she gazed at the thick trees and the young spring grass she wondered again how *anyone* could live anywhere else. After just two semesters of suffering through a continuous bout of homesickness, she returned to the Midwest to continue her studies at the University of Michigan in Ann Arbor. It wasn't at all that she didn't *like* Maine...but after she had spent some time there she realized how very much she adored the true beauty of Michigan.

"Well I guess we've got the peace and tranquility we wanted," she said finally, turning to face her husband. She leaned over and kissed Ron gently, then looked back up at the old lighthouse.

Ron nodded and spoke.

"We sure have got a lot of work to do before this place will be ready for this winter," he said, his eyes returning to scan the decaying building. While they were both certain the abandoned building was repairable, Ron wasn't so sure how long it was going to take. The entire summer could be spent just making the building structurally sound, not to mention renovating the interior of the lighthouse. As it was the building wouldn't provide much shelter from the elements. There were holes in the walls, a missing door, and a large, gaping puncture in the roof, not to mention the fact that the lighthouse had never been insulated properly. It was late May and although the days were beginning to get warmer, the nights could still be chilly, especially on a small island off Michigan's upper peninsula. St. Helena was a small tract by most standards, some two hundred sixty-seven acres total. Though it was rather close to the mainland there were no homes, no summer cabins, no parks or recreation areas. The waters around the island were filled with hidden rocks and underwater obstructions making navigation not impossible but difficult even for the most experienced boaters. Still, a few people ventured to the island now and then for exploring or picnics. But all in all it was a rare foot that traveled the trails or left prints along the sandy shorelines of St. Helena Island.

Ron continued surveying the old structure, his brow furrowing as he gazed from the conical tower to the frail building that was now rapidly falling in on itself. He raised a hand and scratched at the dark stubble on his cheek, not taking his eyes off the old lighthouse.

"This place has really gone to hell," he reiterated. Indeed, it looked as if no one had taken care of the place in a hundred years...which, when it really came down to it, no one had. Ron and Janet had been commissioned by the

International Lighthouse Preservation Society to completely restore the St. Helena Island lighthouse, which had sat alone and desolate for the better part of one hundred years. There had been a few half-hearted attempts at restoration over the years, but so far none that had been successful. Neglect continued to eat away at the wooden window sills and decay feasted on the grayed wood siding. Rot had begun to gnaw at most of the flooring, and years of atrophy weighed heavily on the roof. The rotting boards were a misty, gun-metal gray; lighter in some places, darker in others depending on the level of wood rot. Most of the shingling had long ago slid off the roof, and giant heaps of the disintegrating squares lay in piles around the house. The mounds of shingles were disheveled and clumped like immense piles of decomposing elephant dung. Grass and weeds grew up around and through fallen timbers and crumbled beams. A pair of barn swallows had built a nest under an eve and every minute or so one would appear, either darting back to the nest or scurrying out in search of food. The entire endeavor was to be, as Ron had suspected even before he'd seen it, a *total* restoration project from the ground up. *Everything* needed some repair if not complete replacing.

Except-

Except for the windows.

Years of disregard had wreaked havoc on everything but the windows. All were fully intact without even so much as a crack. Not even the tiny *beginning* of a crack. Ron had curiously checked them out one by one on his initial inspection a few weeks earlier. From a distance it appeared that *all* of the windows had been broken out. But a closer look revealed that the windows were indeed completely intact, and except for a few smudges and cobwebs, they were incredibly undamaged by season after harsh season of unforgiving ice, snow, wind and rain. It seemed amazing that through the years the windows had not suffered any damage not only from the weather, but from the small handful of people that occasionally traveled to the tiny island to explore the old remains.

A breeze rushed across the meadow, tasseling Ron's thick brown hair. At age thirty-six he was just two years older than his wife, but to his dismay most people thought he was a decade older than she. Silver flecks had begun to appear in his hair, and he had worn a beard up until last year when the gray ghost had begun to take up residence there, too. He blamed his premature graying on long days of work, two young children, and maybe a bit too much partying in college. In those days he'd been quite thin; he'd begun to put on more weight these past few years and the makings of a small ATV tire flopped lazily around his mid-section. Living on the island and working on the lighthouse almost every waking moment would give him the opportunity to lose a little bit of that, he hoped. There wouldn't be any twenty-four hour convenience stores or fast-food restaurants to tempt him on the way home from work. Hell...this *was* his home for all practical purposes. Home was now the old building that loomed over him, on a two hundred sixty-seven acre uninhabited island. No electricity, no stores, no neighbors, no television. It would be the opportunity he needed to just forget a few things for a while.

Like death, Ron thought. He lowered his head as the wave of emotion rushed over him again, short-circuiting all of his other thoughts. Not a month had passed since he had buried not one but *both* of his parents, as well as his older brother. The three had been driving back from an anniversary dinner and were hit head on by an oncoming vehicle going the wrong way on Interstate 75. The accident happened at night, and the driver in the oncoming vehicle had been driving without headlights. There had been no warning, no time to react. Just-

Death.

The coroner said that it had been so sudden for all three that there was no way they would have felt anything. Somehow those flat words of assurance didn't make Ron feel much better. The words sounded more like the weekend sports reporter that had the dubious dishonor of telling the viewers at home that their beloved team had lost, but they'd put up a good fight and that was what mattered most. Which sounded very good and noble, but it was a crock of shit either way you looked at it. They lost the game. It didn't matter who played or how well they played. They were losers, if only for a night. And being on the losing team for one night was bad enough for Ron's mother, father, and brother. It was a six hour drive to where his parents lived in Illinois, but he and Janet and the kids made the drive usually once a month. The children had absolutely loved their grandparents and couldn't wait for their all too infrequent visits. Ron's family had always been close, even after he had grown and moved away.

Having a family of his own seemed to tighten the bond. And much to Ron's delight, his parents absolutely adored Janet from the very start. They had liked her the day they had met her and although they didn't say so verbally, they'd always hoped the two would get married. After Ron and Janet eloped, Ron's parents were ecstatic. The news of a grandchild a few years later sent them over the edge with joy, and the birth of Casey two years after Jon might have just as well been heaven on earth.

But now his parents were gone, and a brother as well. No good-byes, no *seeyalater's,* no *catchatamarrow's*...just a phone call in the middle of the night, and a Michigan State Trooper on the other end of the line talking about-

Death.

Oh, the cop had tried to be sensitive about it. *There's been an accident, Mr. Borders...Yes, well...maybe you could meet us here at the hospital. We'll talk more then. And Mr. Borders...I'm sorry....*

The funeral arrangements and the burial left him empty and cold. Ron had always known that the day would come- *some day.* But *Some Day* always seemed so far away. *Some Day* was a season that was supposed to be months and months and years away. It was like that last payment on the mortgage, the final check on the revolving line of credit. Sure and true, its arrival was guaranteed. It would be coming...*Some Day.* But so many days of crystal blue skies and spring flowers had obscured any thoughts of *Some Day* being today or tonight or tomorrow or next week or the next hour or the next minute or second. *Some Day* had arrived, unannounced and uninvited, bringing the future to a sudden, crashing collision with the present. *Some Day* had knocked on the door a few short weeks ago, bringing all of its confusion and shock and disbelief and all the other emotions that Ron *knew* it would...but wasn't quite ready to deal with. He supposed there was probably no way to *really* prepare you for the death of a relative, especially when it came in such a violent, disturbing fashion. No, for the most part, death pretty much had *carte blanche* to arrive whenever it felt like it.

Yes? Mr. Borders? Pleased to meet you. I'm Death. We have this very special introductory offer for you to consider....

Perhaps, Ron thought, the only way it could have been worse would be to watch someone die after years of struggling with an incurable disease or illness. Maybe then it would be more painful to watch the prolonged agony of someone who could do nothing about their condition but nod their head and eat syrup and blended fruit for the duration of their days. And even then he questioned if anybody could *really* be prepared or ready for what was most obviously inevitable and unavoidable.

Death.

Some Day.

Someday.

Maybe, just maybe, by focusing completely on the restoration of the old structure, *Some Day* could be forgotten for just a little while. Maybe a task such as this would do the trick, simply by concentrating entirely on the project at hand. When it came right down to it, Ron admitted he knew relatively little, if anything, about lighthouses. In fact, he hadn't *planned* on a career as a builder or a carpenter in the first place. He had gone to the University of Michigan and was pursuing a degree in dentistry before he lost total interest, managing to complete two full semesters and part of a third before dropping out. Actually, it wasn't necessarily losing interest as much as it was *diverting* his interest elsewhere. While in school, he and Janet bought an old shack of a farmhouse just outside of Traverse City. This was back in the early eighties before property in the Grand Traverse region had hit the financial twilight zone. They bought the old house and two acres for a mere $10,000 with plans of just fixing it up to have a vacation home. They traveled north from Ann Arbor every Friday to work on the old house, returning Sunday evening. It wasn't long before they began leaving for Traverse City on Thursday evening and returning on Monday morning. Soon what had started out as a simple hobby became an obsession. Ron began missing quite a bit of school to stay up north and work on restoring the home. Neither he nor Janet had much experience and the project had taken a few years, but the results were impressive: they sold the fully restored home and the small amount of acreage for $140,000.

So, for the next few years, that was what they did: looked for old homes, dumps that were gold mines just waiting to be harvested. It was tough work. Long hours, late nights, and always exceeding even the most carefully thought-out budget. But it was worth it to both. They loved restoring the old homes, took their time, and learned along the way. One day Janet found a small classified ad in

Michigan Homes Magazine. The ad simply read:

**WANTED: International Lighthouse
Preservation Society is seeking a
person or persons to restore
lighthouse facility on St. Helena
Island. Call Harry at (616) 555-2000.**

After much discussion between himself and Janet, Ron finally called to find out more about the job. The ILPS was very thorough, and by no means were they going to hire the first people who came along. The Society Chairman wanted detailed references and photos of homes that they had restored. Then, and only then, were they offered the job. Ron and Janet rented a small boat to ferry them to St. Helena to see the lighthouse first hand and to see what they would be getting in to should they accept the offer. The light that hadn't been operational since the early 1900's and the condition of the building, they had been warned, was deplorable. The pay wasn't going to be great, and they would make substantially less than they would if they were to restore a home and sell it. But the offer sounded... *convincing.* An island in Lake Michigan, overlooking the Mackinac Bridge and the entire Straits region. *'Fix it up, take your time...well, not all your time,'* the chairman had said. The International Lighthouse Preservation Society had grants to restore a number of lighthouses that were in disrepair, and the St. Helena light was one of the worst. But Ron and Janet fell in love with the island and the quaint old home instantly, despite its condition. Ron had called Harry that same night.

It was to be, as Ron first put it, a meager living at best. No power or telephone. No e-mail. No neighbors. Just an old boat with an outboard motor to travel the two miles to the mainland. In fact, if the waves were over two feet, which they often were in Lake Michigan, the boat would be useless. For all practical purposes they would remain on the island all the time, except on rare occasions when they would go for food or emergencies. Ron and Janet had decided that a trip about once a month would be all that was needed, provided they were able to get all of their supplies in one trip. Naturally, all food would have to be carefully purchased, as there would be no way to keep anything refrigerated. At least until the colder fall and winter months, when they would be able to put away frozen meat for a wonderful treat now and then. A two way radio would provide their only means of contact with the world. Ron had initially packed an AM/FM radio, thought twice about it and finally decided to leave it behind. But of course it wouldn't be like they were totally alone. Many boats sailed the waters often. There were fishermen out for the days' catch, sailboats cruising through the Straits, and even large freighters that lumbered through the waters four or five times a day. It wouldn't be like they were cut off completely from civilization, but for the most part they would have the peace and quiet that they had always dreamed of. And it might give them both...even Casey and Jon...a chance to put a few things behind them.

Some Day.

The children had been delighted with the idea. Not having to attend school thrilled Jon, and Casey was still too young to know whether or not she had enjoyed attending kindergarten. Janet would 'lighthouse' school the children during the time spent on the island. After the lighthouse was fully restored they planned to find someplace more permanent to live. By then Jon would be ten or eleven, Casey would be eight or nine, and the two would need to be around children their age and begin developing friendships of their own. Neither Ron nor Janet had any idea where they would settle for sure. Perhaps in Michigan's western upper peninsula, still scenic and wild and forested. Or maybe northern Wisconsin where Janet's parents now lived. They had a lot of choices, but none they had to even think about soon...unless it involved the lighthouse.

A loud shriek diverted his thoughts, and Ron and Janet both snapped their heads towards the sound just in time to catch a glimpse of six-year old Casey splash headlong into ankle-deep water. She jumped up in an instant, smiling and sputtering, laughing and giggling with delight. The cold waters were no match for her vibrant spirit and zest for excitement. Even her brother Jon, her elder by two years, wasn't nearly as outgoing and energetic as his little sister. It was Casey who was the bold one, always egging Jon to do something, always fearless, never tired. Casey could play for hours immersed and engrossed totally in the moment, enjoying every minute of whatever she was doing, wherever she was doing it. She was talkative and gregarious, which was in stark contrast to her brother. While Jon was not at all a quiet, shy boy, her sister's overactive exuberance seemed a direct conflict to his easy-going, introspective nature. Jon was compellingly curious, and could spend hours-if not an entire *day*-catching various types of beetles and watching them clamor through an old mayonnaise jar stuffed with a few green leaves and sticks he had gathered. Casey would show intense interest in the tiny insects for only a few moments before becoming bored and searching out new activities to satisfy her appetite for fun.

"Casey! Jon!" Janet called. The two children left the shoreline and bounced through the line of cedars and evergreens that encroached the lake. Casey was entirely soaked, her sun-bleached blonde hair stuck to her round, rosy-red cheeks, water rolling off her shoulders. Jon had not remained unscathed, as evidenced by the dark blue water line than stopped just short of the knees of his new Levi's. Both were smiling and running as they ran through the small cluttered field that at one time been a front yard. Thick underbrush had begun to grow up through unkept grass, only adding to the loneliness of the lighthouse that had been dark for a long, long time.

One by one, they came out.

Casey and Jon sat cross-legged in awe and amazement as the number of fireflies began to grow by the second. The evening campfire had died down, the plump hot dogs had been devoured, and Ron and Janet carefully held two green switches over the dying orange embers, roasting the last of the evening's marshmallows. An orchestra of crickets serenaded in harmonious perfection, conducted by the occasional booming of a bullfrog somewhere near the lake. The moon was absent and stars blanketed the heavens above. More fireflies were appearing and the two children sat motionless, mesmerized by the tiny dots of light that filled the young six-inch high grass and swarmed through the night sky. Even Ron and Janet were struck by the beauty of the fireflies. Their tiny, glowing bodies blinked like miniature neon lights in an otherwise pitch-black field.

Suddenly Jon sprang to his feet.

"I'm gonna get some!" he announced, and he bounded up from the log he had been seated on. Instantly his sister bolted up and followed after him. *"Wait for me! Wait for me!"* she cried. Jon picked up an old bottle he had found earlier in the day and the two children quickly disappeared into the myriad of tiny blinking flames, and the chorus of crickets was soon joined by the shrill cries of *I got one!* and *here's one!* The two children bounded about happily, unseen in the dark meadow.

Ron pulled Janet closer as he withdrew his marsh-mallow from over the coals, popping the lightly-browned egg-sized ball of goo into his mouth. It crunched as he chewed and now Janet raised her stick as well, pulling the hot marshmallow from the thin limb and placing it on a portable table next to her where it would soon be gobbled up by either Casey or Jon. Neither of the children had much luck roasting marshmallows themselves as Jon was far too infatuated with watching the white ball burst into a brilliant blue and yellow torch, and Casey always seemed to drop the mallow into the coals where it emerged as an inedible black and gray gooey ball of ashes.

"Care for some?" Ron asked, as he fumbled in the darkness for a bottle of Chardonnay that sat in the grass near him. Janet nodded her head and mumbled an enthusiastic *mmmhmmph* as she finished the rest of a marshmallow. Ron poured the wine into two foam cups that had served them well throughout the day and handed one to Janet.

"Cheers" she said, and the two would-be wine glasses made a slight swishing sound as they touched. "And not a bad selection to go with marshmallows," she added after a small sip.

Branches cracked and snapped and Casey reappeared in the firelight, her eyes glossed over, fighting back tears.

"Mom...Jonny caught my firebug," she complained. "I was tryin' to catch him and Jonny grabbed him." Her bottom lip began to tremble and she looked as if she would burst out crying at any moment.

"Oh, no he didn't, sweetie. Look...there he is right there." Janet pointed to one of nearly a half-dozen fireflies that were buzzing only a few feet from where Casey stood. Instantly she was off again, the minor crisis passed.

Ron stood up, setting his foam cup on the ground. "I'll be right back," he said. "Nature calls." He began walking across the dark field towards the lighthouse.

"I'll be glad when we can both answer its call without stepping into the bushes," Janet called after him, smiling.

"It's a little easier for *you* than it is for *me*." There was no power on the island and wouldn't be for some time, if at all. The ILPS had promised they would provide them with a gas generator, but they said that it was going to take at least a week and maybe longer before it arrived. Some back order or something. Until then, all restroom facilities would be courtesy of the thick line of brush and trees on the south side of the lighthouse, near the edge of Lake Michigan. There had once been a tiny privy situated behind the lighthouse, but now it was in such poor condition that they wouldn't dare attempt to use it.

Even with the blazing stars in the sky the night was very dark, and all that could be seen were the silhouettes of the treetops as they stretched upward towards the heavens. The dark form of the lighthouse rose above him, silent and shadowy and black in the chilly evening. The drone of crickets filled his ears reminding Ron of a childhood of his own, long past and now only a distant memory like some slow moving freight train chugging along the tracks. As a boy he had spent many summer nights at a small cabin near Burt Lake, and now the sights and smells and sounds of St. Helena Island took him back there again, back to a time when he, like Casey and Jon, had run playfully through a dark field, leaping high into the air to gather fireflies from the night sky. Summers were golden then, and the nights were filled with mystery and wonder. Everything was safe and perfect and the days were filled with excitement and adventure. Those days had slipped away like billowing white clouds, drifting overhead and passing quickly by, finally creeping over the horizon to be gone forever. Once in a while Ron would catch a glimpse of those moments, if only a fleeting glance, through the eyes of his children. Jon and Casey reminded him that the days of his own youth hadn't been merely a dream, that they had been *real*, and they existed today in his own fond memories...and in the joyous laughter and delighted smiles of his children.

He paused for a moment to let his eyes adjust to the dark before venturing any further along the side of the lighthouse. After a few moments and some careful steps, he was able to locate the old path that would serve as an open hallway to their modest evergreen latrine. A thick carpet of last year's pine needles crunched beneath his shoes and small branches swished against his denim jeans as he made his way slowly to the dark tree line. Behind him the form of the lighthouse rose into the night sky, its black form emerging from the shadows and blotting out the starry pavilion.

He stood on the shoreline on the other side of the trees, relieving himself as he looked over the waters of Lake Michigan. About seven miles to the east the span of the Mackinac Bridge was easily visible, lit up brightly in the night sky. The longest suspension bridge in the world connected Michigan's mainland to the upper peninsula. Or connected the upper peninsula to the mainland, depending on which side of the bridge you lived. If you were south of the bridge and lived on the lower peninsula, you were branded a *'Troll'* by those living in the upper peninsula. And those in the upper were likewise dubbed *'Yoopers,'* a name that was worn with pride by all who could lay claim to it. And the Mackinac Bridge, some Yoopers felt, wasn't always a *good* thing. It made it too easy for a Troll invasion with their campers and hunting gear and ORV's and snowmobiles and other noisemakers that continued to assault the pristine wilderness of the upper peninsula season after season. But the influx of tourists brought cash, and quite a large population of the upper peninsula was sustained by tree-hungry, space-loving, money-flaunting Trolls. Even the Mackinac Bridge itself had been a tourist destination for many and was almost always lit up like a Christmas tree year round, with brilliant amber lights strung along the suspension cables and up the towering tiers. Ron could see the slow moving microscopic headlights of cars as they made their way over the span at a whopping forty-five miles per hour. At the southern end of the bridge the bright lights of Mackinaw City fluttered and twinkled, and if Ron had been inside the light at the top of the conical tower all points of the mainland including the Bridge, Mackinac Island, Mackinaw City, and even a few other islands far to the south would be visible on a clear night such as this.

His bladder now empty and his eyes acclimated to his surroundings, he had no problem finding the short trail that wound back to and along side the old lighthouse. He crept quietly beneath the weathered structure and stopped.

Behind the lighthouse at the edge of the meadow, Janet was leaning near the edge of the orange coals. Jon and Casey were there, and the three were huddled around the campfire watching the luminous glow emanating from the old bottle. The bottle sat on the portable folding card table and Ron could see the dark silhouette of his son as he held his hand over the top of the glass, keeping the tiny insects from escaping. They had caught dozens of fireflies...so many that the children's faces seemed to glow in the green-orange light. Behind them, the darkened field and the sky above was still aflame with thousands of the tiny sparks that had somehow eluded captivity. The lucky ones were safe; at least until tomorrow night when once again Casey and Jon would be sure to begin their hunting and gathering of the flying bugs. Ron smiled, again remembering partaking in the exact same activity as a child. Catching fireflies had been a highlight of summer nights until he was ten. Then the highlight changed to hunting until he was thirteen...then his attention was drawn to girls. At sixteen, Ron figured it out: *hunt* for *girls.*

He turned to look at the aging lighthouse behind him. A century ago someone had lived here, keeping the place in order, carefully maintaining the light which would help guide ships through the often treacherous stretch of water that wound through the Straits of Mackinac. Someone had lived here year round, perhaps with their family...perhaps even with children...to care for and keep the lighthouse in fine working condition, making a home out of the otherwise lonely, desolate dwelling. It was a cheerless existence, taking care of a lighthouse so far from any major city. Even a hundred years ago the Straits had been a booming region, filled with lumber ships and traders peddling their goods. The Straits of Mackinac was a thoroughfare for ships on their way to and from Chicago, New York, Detroit, Toledo, and all points in between. But St. Helena Island was excluded from most of the major traffic. A small fishing village had once thrived, but the shallow waters around the island kept most larger ships away, far out into the Straits and in deeper waters. There really hadn't been any port or anything like it on the island, just a long dock that extended out from shore. But the lighthouse at the southern tip of the island was of major importance, helping to guide ships through the Straits and assisting in their navigation of the treacherous, shoal-filled waters. There were dozens upon dozens of shipwrecks in the Straits area alone, most from a time before modern technology. A time when you had to guess the weather for the coming week or two, and if you guessed wrong...well, that was just too bad. The hulking remains of the giant freighter *Cedarville* slumbered somewhere in the dark waters beneath the Mackinac Bridge, struck by another ship in dense fog back in 1965. Ten men had been lost in that disaster alone; there were thousands of other men and women that had met similar fates in the Great Lakes over the past two hundred years. Somewhere beneath the bridge was rumored to be the wreck of the schooner *Falcon.* The ship was lost during a violent storm in 1841, carrying a fortune in diamonds. The vessel was said to have been lost in the Laurentian Channel, which was an extremely deep crevice that twisted its way through the Straits and down in to Lake Huron. The channel was said to reach depths of over six hundred feet; far beyond the limit of sport divers. Hundreds of treasure hunters from around the country and even around the world had scoured the Straits for years in search of the vast fortune. Three men had even lost their lives in vain searching for the long lost wreckage. Wherever in the

Straits she lay, one thing was certain: if the wreck of the ill-fated *Falcon* was lost in the Laurentian Channel with her dangerous depths and unpredictable currents, neither the ship nor its cargo would be salvaged anytime soon.

Ron started walking towards the campfire, then turned back and glanced up at the old structure behind him.

At first he didn't notice it, but then he stopped and looked again. There was something strange...something that just wasn't quite right about the appearance of the old building. But what it was he couldn't quite put his finger on.

That's odd, he thought, facing the darkened structure. He looked at a window of the lighthouse and then back towards his wife and children. The three were still hovered around the glowing bottle, laughing and giggling. Even Janet seemed rather amused at the amount of fireflies Casey and Jon had captured. Their faces radiated in the glow of the dying fire.

He looked back at the window...or rather, *through* the window...and then turned again to look at the thousands of fireflies dancing in the dark field. Again, he turned to look at the window.

There's no reflection, he thought. *There's no reflection in the glass at all.*

He stepped closer to the window, squinting in the darkness to see a hint of light that should reflect at least *a little* bit of the sparks of light in the field...certainly the glowing bottle on the table and the embers of the fire.

Nothing, he thought. *There's absolutely no reflection in the window.* He looked over at another window and it too was strangely absent of any reflection. He looked up at the shape of the huge lantern room that housed the light at the top of the conical tower. Once again the glass displayed no reflection of fireflies, stars, whatever. All of the windows were completely black. A black so dark that even his adjusted eyes couldn't pick out any forms or shapes or images at all. He stood frozen, rigid and straight, staring at the window.

The empty black square called to him, as if beckoning him to enter. The darkness was like an abyss, an endless cavern with no end. Ron stared curiously into the depths of the blackness, no beginning, no end, just-

Nothing.

He took a slow step forward, glancing down cautiously before his foot reached the ground. The area close to the building was littered with debris, and he would need to watch his footing as he approached. He peered into the darkness, glancing back once again to see Janet and Casey and Jon huddled around the table, still delighted with the fireflies in the jar. Ron turned back to face the lighthouse and lifted his arm up and looked at his watch, twisting his wrist. But it wasn't the *time* that mattered. He tilted the watch until he could see the small glass dome.

There.

The light was faint, but it was there all right. Very tiny dots, one larger and more orange than the rest, appeared on the glass dome of his watch. He held his arm up, staring at the reflection of the campfire in the glass of his watch. Once again, his eyes focused on the window before him.

Still nothing.

The window remained completely void of any light whatsoever. It looked more like a piece of black carbon paper that a window. He squinted in the darkness, but it was impossible to see inside the building. The glass square before him resembled more of a pit...a long, horizontal well that went on for ever and ever. An odd feeling came over him and he felt as if he *were* indeed staring down, that somehow the laws of gravity had been repealed and he was now floating over a deep, dark hole, floating weightless, looking down into the depths of eternity.

He took another step forward and stumbled on an old rotting board that had been laying in wait for years, perhaps waiting just for this moment. He felt a sting in his foot as the nail punctured his shoe.

"*Son of a bitch,*" he cursed beneath his breath. "*Smart Ron...really smart.*" He recoiled and pulled his foot back up and freed his shoe from the nail. The pain faded quickly as the nail had just barely pierced the tender skin. He set his foot back down gently, paying closer attention this time. He glanced back up at the window.

A face.

It had only been a flash...a short, flickering afterimage that appeared only for an instant...but his reflection had appeared in the window. Or he had *thought*. No...he was *sure* of it. But the impression had quickly snapped away, leaving the window just as it had been...dark, cold, and-

Lifeless.

He shuffled still closer, picking up his feet slowly and cautiously, his steps deliberate and smooth. His eyes remained focused on the ominous black chasm before him.

The old, feeble structure loomed high above him and just a few yards to the south the spiraling conical tower rose upward, hiding the stars and concealing the night sky.

Ron was now close enough to touch the window. He reached out cautiously, ever so slowly...pausing for just an instant...then dragged his finger along the smooth glass.

It was if someone had turned on a television. The black, foreboding hole disappeared and the window sprang to life. The fuzzy, distant images of the field behind him materialized instantly in the pane before him. In the window he could now see the field aflame with fireflies. They were like thousands of lit matches, each one igniting, burning out, then igniting again. The reflections of the twinkling insects and the dying embers of the fire were crisp and clear in the glass. Above and around, the other windows reflected the same scene. Ron turned and looked again at the three distant figures still huddled around the folding card table. They were laughing and talking, captivated by the glowing bottle of bugs. Behind them, covering the meadow and trees and frolicking in the sky blinked hundreds of tiny night-lights: on, off; on again, off again. Ron slowly turned his gaze back to the window, and the reflected scene remained unchanged.

Suddenly, the crickets stopped chirping. A light breeze slithered through the trees, and the St. Helena lighthouse, long abandoned and forgotten for so many, many years, took a long, lumbering breath.

And stirred once again.

CHAPTER TWO

Warm breath and a gentle in and out whooshing of air greeted Ron as he awoke. Casey had been trying to wake him up and she peered curiously over him, her bright six-year old face only inches from her slumbering father. She reached up with tiny fingers and pried one of Ron's eyes open.

"Daddy...? Daddy wake up...Daddy...?" Ron waited a few moments longer, just long enough to allow Casey to believe that he was still sleeping. Then with a sudden burst he wrapped his arms around his daughter and pulled her

close, much to the delight of the surprised Casey. He held her tightly as she wriggled in his grasp, laughing and giggling. It was a game they often played and one Casey delighted in.

"Daddy!" she giggled. Janet was awake now as well, and she rolled over in the sleeping bag and snuggled closer to her husband. Casey had already escaped from her father and was urging both parents out of the tent, suddenly remembering what she had awoke her father for. Her blue eyes grew wide and her puffy red cheeks swelled as she opened her mouth to speak.

"It's a *slug!"* she exclaimed. "Jonny found a slug on his sleeping bag! Come quick!!" The canvas flap snapped open and closed and she was gone, hurriedly rushing back to the tent she was sharing with her brother. Ron had decided that at least until the lighthouse was cleaned up a bit that they would be spending their nights in the Coleman tents they had packed. It would be too dangerous fumbling at night through an old home that they were unfamiliar with. And although the Borders' Family Camping Trips numbered at least eight per year, this was the first time that the children had spent the night in their own tent. The night had gone by without incident.

"She probably wants to cook it for breakfast," Ron moaned groggily as he ran his fingers through his hair. He rubbed the sleep from his eyes and turned to face his wife. Janet kissed his neck and smiled.

"No," she replied, snuggling closer. "I'm afraid she'll probably want to keep it for a pet."

Breakfast of eggs, bacon, orange juice and hash browns was devoured by all but Casey, who spent most of her time watching the finger-sized dark brown slug inch its way up and down and back and forth inside a glass baby food jar. Jon, after a few minutes of observation and consideration, lost interest in the slug. Casey was pleased to become its new legal guardian, a task she took very seriously.

"Squiggy," she said in proud youthful satisfaction. "I'm gonna call him Squiggy."

"That's a stupid name for a slug," Jon chipped in, and that started an array of sniping and verbal jabbing between the two children that lasted the better part of the morning. Ron and Janet spent the hours assessing the structure of the lighthouse, making notes as to what would have to be done first, where the real trouble spots were, and what it would take to repair them. They were both eager to begin, but careful planning would be needed before any work could be started. For the next few days, most work would consist of careful surveys and notes on paper as they began to estimate what would need to be done first, what materials they would need and how much...which presented another problem. The ILPS had promised to ship over a supply of lumber and other materials within a few weeks, but there was bound to be other odds and ends that they would need for the project. There was no way to just run down to the hardware store and pick up a box of nails or anything that might have been forgotten on their monthly trip to the mainland. They couldn't afford to overlook even the smallest of items, as a trip to St. Ignace in the small motorboat was a lengthy excursion. They wouldn't have the time to run back and forth to the small town more than once per month, if that. Indeed, to call the restoration of the St. Helena Island lighthouse a mere *challenge* would be an underestimation.

The late morning sun bathed the tiny island in glorious warmth. The damp, green grass dried slowly, and cold droplets of dew were soon gobbled up by the steadily rising temperatures. The pristine blue waters of Lake Michigan played calmly at the shore, licking at the sand and rocks and tickling the small pebbles and stones that had washed up along the beach. Seagulls that had spent the night huddled on the sand were now taking to the air to begin another day of scavenging for food. A large dead fish had washed ashore overnight and a dozen gulls fought and jockeyed for position at the table, each bird lunging forward and back, screaming and screeching, pecking and pulling at the dead fish before being chased away by another gull. On the roof of the lighthouse a squirrel suspiciously eyed the four intruders at the edge of the meadow. When it saw two of the unknown invaders approaching it scurried off quickly, leaping expertly from the roof to a nearby branch and running to safety high within the large tree. Jon and Casey were still busy exploring the field and Ron and Janet carefully walked across the warped boards of the porch of the lighthouse.

"Be careful where you step," Ron warned as the front door clunked slowly open. The lock had given out long ago and the many scars and bruises on the wood were evidence that the door had been kicked in more than once.

Janet snapped a few more photos from the front of the porch while Ron scouted the ground floor of the lighthouse. The old building creaked and moaned, whining and crying out with every step. The air was heavy and damp, and with every breath Ron's lungs felt thick and full. He walked slowly through the house and exited out the door of the summer kitchen.

The conical tower stood towering in the sky, gray and dirtied from years of inattention. A number of bricks had fallen from their places and lay scattered about on the ground, left broken and crumbling at the base of the tower. A dozen or so seagulls sat complacently at the top of the light, their feathers fluttering and ruffling in the wind as they eyed Ron keenly with wariness and suspicion. At that elevation the wind was quite a bit stronger than it was near the ground mainly because the tower was completely in the open, standing up to the fiercest of Lake Michigan winds throughout the year. A burly steel padlock kept the door of the tower secured and had done so for many years. The view from atop the lighthouse was spectacular and as Ron dug for the old key in his pocket he thought about climbing up for a quick check, then opted to wait until both he and Janet, as well as Casey and Jon, could join in. The kids were sure to love the view and he couldn't wait to see their faces as they reached the top and looked out over the beautiful blue waters, the bridge, and the distant mainland.

Ron turned to face the old building. A line of weeds and shrubs grew up all around the house, choking the stone foundations. He pulled at the smaller ones and met with some success, but some of the bigger shrubs had grown too big and were going to take a hatchet or a hand saw to remove them. He grasped a cedar sapling with both hands and pulled. The small tree held fast to the ground, but as Ron pulled harder he could hear the smaller roots begin to snap and pop beneath the sod. The immature sapling had grown tightly against the old rocks and stones, perhaps even into the foundation itself. The tree budged slowly, inching upward as he continued pulling. Suddenly the young cedar broke away, surprising Ron and causing him to lose his balance and stumble back. He caught himself before he fell, still grasping the sapling with both hands. The root system had left a hole near the stone foundation, and Ron stepped forward to kick the disturbed earth back in to place.

Only then did he notice the window.

It had obviously been there all along, but the branches of the cedar sapling had hidden it well, and the window had been completely concealed by the thick limbs and leafy foliage. Like all of the other windows it was perfect. No chips, cracks, scratches...*nothing.* It was a window to a room downstairs, and as Ron peered through he caught a glimpse of Janet as she walked by the doorway and made her way around the inside of the lighthouse, camera held up to her face, clicking off photographs. But he hardly noticed her or the other objects in the room. It was the *window* he was looking at. Not only was the window in complete pristine condition, but it was *spotless*. There were no water spots, no cobwebs in the corners, no streaks. There didn't even appear to be dust on the glass, either inside or out. The wooden pane was old and gray and completely rotted in some places, but the window itself was immaculate.

Unbelievable, Ron thought as he leaned forward for a closer inspection. The glass was clean and clear, as if it had just been washed or polished. Ron strained to find a mark, any flaw of any-

There.

At the bottom right hand corner, almost invisible. A smudge of some sort. In fact, it *would* be invisible from any other angle, but the light caught it just right from the position Ron was standing. He moved closer still.

Well I'll be damned, he thought, his eyes focusing on the glass before him.

It was a hand print. A perfect hand, a left hand, the size of a man's. Ron could see the wavering lines traveling erratically through the fingers and the deep crevices that crisscrossed the palm area. The lines flowed like a map, creating a maze of thinly woven threads. But the print, like the window, was *too* perfect. It was *too* neat, *too* clean. Fingerprints on glass were usually a bit smudgy from the skin's oil, but this print was more like a carefully defined work of art. He reached up, wiping at it with his shirt sleeve, but the print remained. Ron squinted, edging even closer to the glass. His face was now just inches from the pane.

The print was literally a *part* of the glass. Ron ran his fingernail across the palm print and he could actually feel the minuscule ripples and crevices of the hand. It was as if he were feeling another's skin, only *this* skin was rigid and hard beneath his fingers. It mimicked the appearance of a candle after a finger or hand was pressed to the warm wax, only this was harder and more solid. Ron was curious, wondering how long the old print had been there. Probably from long, long ago when the lighthouse was first being built.

His face was still a few inches from the glass when the maze of lines within the print began to twist and turn. Ron blinked, a look of total disbelief on his face. His eyes grew wide and he opened his mouth as if to speak. The lines of the print were rolling about, wrapping themselves around one another, boiling within the glass hand like a ball of venomous snakes in a pit. Again Ron blinked and his hands flew to his face, rubbing his eyes as if they alone were to be blamed for the trickery. He couldn't believe what he was seeing. He *wouldn't* believe what he was seeing. The writhing lines moved faster, slithering in and around one another.

Slowly...ever so slowly...the entire hand began to move. The index finger quivered a moment, then began to bend sluggishly. Other fingers began to twitch and squirm and now the whole hand was flexing and stretching like it was waking up from a long, deep sleep. Ron continued staring, a horrified expression frozen on his face. The glass had taken on the transparency of cellophane and the bizarre hand began to reach toward him, bending the entire window, stretching from the pane, reaching, reaching....

A sharp, stinging pain in his temple brought his hand up, slapping at the side of his face. A small ball crunched against his skin, and then another piercing jab struck his finger. He jumped back and slapped the wasp to the ground and took a few steps away from the structure, his eyes scanning the area for more. Another black wasp buzzed overhead and Ron ducked, his eyes following the flying insect as it made a wide arched loop and lit just a few inches above the window. It crawled about for an instant before disappearing into a small crack in the wood. Soon another wasp appeared in the sky, flying directly to the entrance of the nest, vanishing. Another wasp emerged from the crack and buzzed towards Ron and he ducked again, this time almost falling to the ground on all fours as the insect sped by.

Cripes, he thought. *Gonna have to take care of that. Quick.* A nest of black wasps wasn't something he wanted to screw around with. Two summers previous he and Janet had been working in the attic of an old home when he ran into a nest of ball-faced hornets. They were the meanest, nastiest, ornery animal he had ever encountered. He and Janet suffered nearly a dozen stings on their arms, face and neck, sending them both to the hospital emergency room. A repeat performance was not in his future plans.

He watched as another wasp approached the small

opening and hung suspended in the air for a moment before slithering into the wall. Ron suddenly remembered the hand and once again approached the window, watching the sky for any sign of more wasps. He remained a cars' length away, leaning forward to inspect the window.

The hand was gone. Not only was the hand gone, but it appeared that the entire print was gone as well.

Ron, old buddy...you're crackin' up, he thought, still staring out the window. But he was sure of what he saw. He was about to take another cautious step forward when a wasp buzzed by his head, heading for the nest. There was a lot of insect activity now, and he was surprised that he hadn't noticed the nest before. Like the window, the entrance to the hive had been well hidden by the cedar sapling.

Well, this'll be easy enough, he thought, backing away and making a wide circle back around the nest and to the summer kitchen. He walked back into the lighthouse and found the room with the window, approaching warily to make sure that no wasps had found their way through the walls and inside the house.

The outside of the window was now covered with wasps. Black, buzzing insects crawled up and down, clamoring over one another on the glass. There were dozens and dozens of them swarming about, dancing angrily on the smooth surface. He could hear the faint drone through the window, the reverberation of their wings echoing faintly through the glass. Ron could see their tiny poisonous stingers trailing behind each abdomen like a dangerous sword, ready at any time for a piercing strike.

But the hand print was still gone. Ron searched the area of glass where he had seen it...and he *had* seen it, he told himself. He was certain. But now there was no sign of it at all. The sinister grins of the enraged black wasps glared back at him, their frenzied hum growing louder as the swarm grew larger. The outer side of the window was now completely covered with insects. He made a mental note to make sure that his list of supplies from the mainland would include an industrial size, life-long supply of wasp and hornet killer.

But the hand print. It's gone. It's-

His thought was interrupted by the excited shouts of Jon. Both he and Casey had been playing in the meadow and Ron had heard an occasional unintelligible whoop now and then, but now Jon's shout was much closer.

"Casey!! Come on!! It's a frog!! Help me or he's going to get away!!" Jon's voice came from outside the building, not far from-

"Casey!! Hurry!!"

-the nest.

Ron whirled instantly, grabbing the doorjamb as he spun around the corner, bounding down the hall.

"Jon!" he yelled. *"Get away from the house! Get back to the field!!"* He barged through the summer kitchen and out the door, running around to the north side of the lighthouse.

Jon was standing only a few feet from the window, staring curiously at his father. He held his hands out, one cupped over another. Above and behind him, the window, all the way up to the nest's entrance, was covered with wasps. They swarmed furiously in the air, creating a thick, dark cloud. Ron stopped walking.

"Jon...come here. *Slow.*"

Jon did as he was told, oblivious to the seething blizzard of wasps behind him. When he reached his father Ron squatted down and pointed. Casey had now joined them and the three gazed at the whirling black mist.

"Why are they doing that, Daddy?" Casey asked.

"I don't know, honey. But both of you...*stay away* from this entire side of the house. Understand?" Both children nodded their heads in agreement, and Ron continued. "And keep a close eye out for more. Especially playing in the field. They like to make their nest in old stumps...even in the ground." Both children nodded their heads again. There was a moment of somber silence as the children stared at the swarming wasps. Finally, Jon turned up and looked up at his father, his eyes suddenly bulging with excitement.

"Look at my frog!" he blurted out. He extended his arms up and opened his hands a tiny crack. The frog seized the opportunity and wriggled free, leaping to the ground and bouncing towards the grassy field. Both children bounded after it, running and crouching, lunging forward with their hands, then running again as the frog made its desperate run for the freedom.

Janet appeared in the doorway of the summer kitchen, squinting in the bright sun. The wind blew at her hair and she pulled it away from her face, leaving the camera to dangle from its leather strap around her shoulder.

"Wasps," Ron said, motioning towards the wall. Janet

came towards him and looked at the swarm of insects that covered the wall and window. "I just warned the kids not to go near there. But we're going to have to check for more. There's a lot of places for bees and wasps to build nests around here."

"There's thousands of them," Janet marveled. "What did you do to make them so mad?"

"I didn't clean the sink out after shaving," Ron smirked. Janet turned and looked up into his face, slipping both arms around him now.

"Are you comparing *me* to an angry wasp?" she chided playfully, her smile growing.

"Well, you sure got a pretty cute little stinger," he grinned, swatting her butt. She laughed and slipped her arms around his neck. Ron leaned forward, initiating a brief kiss. Janet drew back after a moment and opened her mouth, speaking in a tone just above a whisper.

"Well, maybe if you're lucky you'll get a little honey later tonight." She smiled and turned away, walking back into the old lighthouse.

Janet loaded another roll of film in the camera and clicked off a few shots of the interior of the summer kitchen. Piles of debris littered the hallways and rooms, and various animals had made nests in walls as well as beneath the floorboards. Ron had gone back to inspecting the outer perimeter of the lighthouse, and she could hear him outside as he organized boards that lay scattered about. She was determined to make sure that every inch of the building had been photographed. It was fun to look back and see how much things had changed as their work progressed, like those before-and-after diet ads that littered the pages of magazines and tabloids. Plus, it would give others a look at just how bad off the lighthouse had been.

Or still is, she corrected herself, stepping over the very old remains of a dead possum. The animal lay on the floor in what appeared to be the pantry. Any odor had long ago faded away, replaced by the dingy, musty smell of rotting wood. The animal lay on its side, its face contorted in one final, anguished grimace of pain. Most of the skin had been eaten away by insects, and what little fur remained was filthy and matted together in clumps. The possum's skull was partially exposed, and sharp incisors jutted from its jaw. A beetle had taken up residence in a cavity that once had been an eye. It would be impossible to know the cause of death, but Janet wasn't really interested in finding out what had brought about the critter's demise. She and Ron often came across dead animals while exploring old buildings and homes. Possums were probably the most common, followed by skunks, then raccoons, squirrels and mice. Usually when humans left the animals moved in, taking over the property for their own. Only sometimes the animals got more than they bargained for. Or less than what they bargained for, depending on how you looked at it. Usually death was caused by ingesting some form of toxic chemical that had been carelessly left laying around. Janet had once watched a raccoon rummaging through the garbage near a cottage in Traverse City. It had scurried off with an empty bottle of window cleaner and she had found the remains of the plastic container the next day, chewed and filled with puncture marks. The raccoon's lifeless body was not far off, an unfortunate victim of poisoning.

Well, maybe we won't take a picture of everything, Janet thought, looking away as she carefully side-stepped the decomposing creature. She slowly made her way back through the hall, looking through the view finder, clicking photos here and there. The walls were absent of any decor and the few furnishings that had survived over the years had been damaged, unfortunately, beyond repair. Even the floor was beginning to give way in some spots, and Janet walked cautiously as she entered into the parlor. The paint on the walls had flaked and peeled for years, and tiny piles of the yellowed, paper-like substance were piled about the floor. What little paint that *did* remain on the walls was cracked and brittle, curling like thin outstretched fingers that were reaching, grasping at the air, at anything, before finally coiling in on themselves. Janet snapped a few shots of the ceiling, the floor, the window, and the front door before returning to the hallway. To her right, an old decrepit staircase lay against the wall like the ancient skeletal remains of a dinosaur. The railing was broken in two and a number of the steps were missing, exposing gaping black holes. She tested the first step, slowly placing her weight on her foot to make sure that it would hold. The stairway protested loudly and cried out in tired despair, but it held fast beneath her weight. The second step she displayed the same caution, and the next one, and the next one. Soon she stood at the top of the stairs on the second floor.

There was a short hallway before her, and four doors, two on each side. Again, she walked cautiously, mindful of her footing. Falling through a rotted floorboard and breaking both of her legs was not something she would enjoy.

The walls and the floors on the second floor were a carbon copy of the first. Old, chipped paint bubbled and cracked on the walls. A portion of the ceiling had caved in over the hallway, revealing a large part of the attic. Above the attic a huge section of the roof had fallen in, tearing open a four-foot hole to expose a bright blue sky. Years of rain had warped the floorboards, twisting the pieces and darkening the curled up, rotting ends. The walls were warped as well, and it reminded Janet of a mirror she had once seen at a circus. The mirror was bent and wavy and when you stood in front of it, images became distorted and deformed. The image would further contort if you backed away from the mirror, making you look smaller or taller.

She took photos of the ceiling, the walls and the doors, slowly making her way around the upstairs. All the doors were closed and appeared to be locked. Janet tested one of the doorknobs. Although it turned in her hand, decades of withstanding the elements had caused the door to warp, freezing it into position. She tried another door, a bit more forceful this time. With a loud, defiant squeak it finally gave way, chugging and creaking slowly open for the first time in many, many years.

The room was empty save for a broken chair and a dozen old beer bottles tossed about. The floor seemed to be in better shape, as it didn't appear to have been exposed to the elements like the hallway had been. The walls were a very ugly shade of light green...a color that looked as if it had grown lighter over the passage of time. Janet stepped inside and clicked off a few photos before exiting and pulling the door closed behind her. She reached for the next door and grasped the knob.

She stopped, slowly removing her hand, staring peculiarly at the knob.

"Ron?" she called out curiously, not taking her eyes from the door. Ron responded by hollering something unintelligible from just outside the summer kitchen.

"C'mere and look at this, honey," she called out again, louder this time. She heard footsteps downstairs, and the methodic *creak crick creack* as Ron carefully crept up the stairs. He found his wife crouched over, studying something on the door.

"What is it?" he asked, peering at the area she was looking at.

"This doorknob. Look at it."

Ron stepped closer and he too crouched down, squinting in the dim light. Although it was mid-afternoon and the sun streamed through the hole in the roof, the upstairs was still quite dark.

"Yeah," he responded, matter-of-factly. "So it's a door knob."

"Ron...look at it.　It's brand new."

Much to the delight of Casey and Jon the fireflies appeared once again in all their glory, first one, then three, then a dozen more, then hundreds. The two children again spent the late evening hours bounding through the open field, snatching firefly after firefly and carefully keeping them all contained in the confines of the bottle Jon had found the day previous. Near midnight, their energy consumed, the two children fell asleep in the laps of their parents next to the dying embers of the evening fire. Ron carried Casey to the tent and tucked her in her sleeping bag and did the same with Jon. The night air was crisp and refreshingly clean and clear, and the thick, creamy trail of the milky way wound high above them in the dark sky. Deep within the island the haunting, lonely calls of a Great Horned Owl echoed through the swamp, joined by the occasional throaty cry of a nighthawk swooping over the dark meadow. Janet tossed two more maple logs on the fire and she and Ron sat on the ground next to one another, sipping the last of the Chardonnay from the same foam cups that were now beginning to show their wear. Ron leaned over and kissed Janet's neck and took another small sip of wine. Janet sipped hers and spoke.

"Find any more wasps today?" she asked.

"No," Ron replied, shaking his head. "There's a nest of yellow jackets in a birch tree down by the water, though. I'll show Jon and Casey where it is tomorrow so they're aware of it. But I don't think that particular one is going to be a problem as long as we stay away from the nest and leave them alone." He motioned towards Janet's camera bag on the card table.

"How many shots did you get?"

Janet raised her eyebrows and pulled a lock of hair behind her ear.

"Three rolls, believe it or not. I made sure to take a lot of pictures of each room as well as outside. I'd like to get some pictures of the inside of the tower as well."

"Yeah, we'll open that up in a day or so. I can't wait to see the kids' faces when they get their first look from the top of the tower. But our first priority is to get at least a portion of the lighthouse in some sort of functioning order...or at least good enough so that we don't have to sleep in these tents, anyway. The ILPS said they would have some supplies shipped over in a few weeks. By then I'd like to be able to give him a good idea of all of the materials we'll need and about how long it'll take to fix this thing up."

There was single swallow of Chardonnay left in the bottle and Ron poured it into Janet's cup. He spoke again as he set the bottle back on the card table.

"Well, I know that there's no power at the lighthouse," he began, nudging closer to his wife. "And we don't even have a generator yet...but what do you say we head over there and maybe try to turn something on?"

"Depends on what the electrician has in mind," Janet said slyly, smirking as she took another sip of wine.

"No harm in trying to find a socket, doncha think?" Ron offered. Janet laughed and leaned closer, gazing into Ron's eyes.

"As long as you promise not to short-circuit me," she whispered, smiling.

Ron chuckled and raised his palm.

"Scout's honor," he replied honestly, not missing a beat.

"What about the kids?" Janet asked, gesturing towards the tent with her foam cup.

"They'll be fine," Ron replied, making a waving motion with his hand. "We'll only be a hundred feet away."

The old door creaked open, and a cold breeze exhaled from the doorway, brushing past the two dark figures.

"Geez it's dark," Ron whispered. "Have you got that candle?"

Janet fumbled in her pockets for the small box of one-inch wood matches she used to light the campfire. The candle burst to life and eerie shadows sprang from their hiding places, dancing in the single flare. Dark corners and crevices slunk warily away, lingering just beyond the flickering candlelight.

"This is kind of spooky," Janet whispered, looking around.

"Oh, come on. You say that every time we make love in an old house." Over the years it had become customary to 'christen' the new homes that they restored. This type of playful consummation added an element of mystery and mischievousness that a simple bed didn't always provide.

"Yeah...but at least *most* houses have electricity," Janet continued. "And usually there's houses all around. Here, we're out in the middle of nowhere...on an island, for gosh sakes." She paused and looked around the room, glancing at the staircase and to the darkened area upstairs. "And I still would like to know how that doorknob got there. I mean...don't you think that's kind of weird? I mean...an old, run down lighthouse...with a *new doorknob?*"

Ron opened another bottle of wine he had brought and refilled their cups. Janet spread a blanket on the floor, mindful of making sure not to lay it over any broken boards.

"I told you. The crew from the Preservation Society probably installed it when they were here last month. Remember Harry said that they were about to start restoring the lighthouse themselves anyway." It was true that members of the Preservation Society had been there on a few occasions earlier in the spring. That could explain the doorknob and the immaculate condition of the windows. Ron found it puzzling that someone would go through the trouble to clean the windows when there was so much other work to be done. But it didn't explain the hand print in the window earlier in the day. He hadn't told Janet about it, and had no plans to do so. Now, after he'd thought about it over the afternoon, he wasn't sure himself exactly what he'd seen.

"I'm sure that they had brought a few things over and started to fix things up a bit," he continued.

"Well, yeah, but-"

Janet hadn't been able to finish her sentence as Ron put his finger gently to her lips. He pulled her t-shirt up over her head, exposing her bare breasts. The shirt fell to the floor and Ron pulled her close, taking one breast in his hand and massaging the soft nipple with his index finger.

"Yeah but nothing," he whispered. Their mouths met and they slowly fell to their knees and onto the blanket.

A single, heavy pound thundered through the entire lighthouse, shattering the quiet stillness and waking both Janet and Ron immediately. Ron sat up on the makeshift bed on the hardwood floor and Janet propped herself up on her elbows. Both listened intently. Outside in the darkness, a thousand crickets and hundreds of peeper frogs chimed in unison.

Pound.

There it was again. It was loud and solid and shook the

walls of the parlor. A few paint chips could be heard as they crumbled from the wall and fell to the wood floor, dislodged by the heavy thump.

"What is it?" Janet whispered nervously.

Without answering, Ron fumbled for his clothes and stood up. He could see nothing as he peered through the window except for the faint outline of dark trees against a star-filled, moonless sky.

Pound. The tremor was louder this time, like a sudden lumbering thunderclap. The ensuing reverberation echoed down darkened halls and unseen rooms. The unexpected burst caused Janet's whole body to jump as she lay on the floor. Even Ron jumped, shaken by the abrupt boom. The noise seemed to be coming from outside of the house, but then again-

Pound.

-it might be in the very next room. Ron cautiously waded through the inky darkness with both of his arms outstretched, fumbling on the table and finally finding the candle and the box of matches. A short scrape was heard as the match head struck the gritty paper on the side of the box and the sulphur exploded to life, once again bathing the room in an eerie, yellow glow. Shadows frolicked and flirted about, swaying to and fro as Ron lit the small vanilla candle. He stepped towards the window, relieved to see the reflection of the candle glowing as he approached the glass. He held the candle out before him, almost touching the clear window. Shadows flew about the room and Janet lay motionless on the floor, watching with her eyes wide, clutching the thin blanket over her breasts. Ron looked at

his reflection in the glass.

No. That can't....

His reflection in the window glared coldly back at him...only...it wasn't *him*.

Ron raised the candle.

I don't look like that. That's...that's not me....

The man in the window didn't budge. Ron's face was replaced with wicked, tormented features. The face in the window was much older...much *much* older than Ron...with harrowing lines streaming down his cheeks and dark, menacing eyes. An evil, twisted grin sneered back at him. It was the face of a madman, of someone who had gone completely insane. He glared back at Ron with a haughty arrogance as if proud to display the fact that indeed he *was* crazy.

That's not me, he said again to himself, shaking his head. As he did so, the reflection in the glass remained poised and motionless. The figure outside of the window didn't move.

The pound on the glass came so suddenly that Ron jumped, dropping the candle. Instantly it was dark again as the flame went out. Janet screamed and Ron leapt back, ready to attack the unknown foe.

"What is it?!?!? Who is it?!?!?" Janet cried.

"Shhh!!" Ron hissed. The two fell silent for what seemed like an eternity.

Seconds passed. Not a word was spoken.

Then-

Footsteps. Footsteps could be clearly heard running away from the lighthouse, tromping heavily through the grass and brush.

"Who's here?!?!" Janet whispered loudly. Ron didn't have the time to answer. In their tents, Casey and Jon had begun to scream and Ron bounded out the door and flew across the dark field.

"Well, ya just never know. Ya just *never* know." Sheriff Deputy Thomas Pearson lifted his hat back and ran his fingers through his thinning dark brown hair as he spoke. Unable to catch up with or find the intruder, Ron had finally radioed the authorities late in the night but the Mackinaw County Sheriff's Department hadn't been able to get anybody to the island until morning. It had been a sleepless night for Ron and Janet, save for the hour or so they had fallen asleep in the lighthouse before being awakened by the loud banging.

Deputy Pearson was a small man with a stocky build on a short frame. He wasn't going to win any hundred-yard dashes, but if push came to shove the deputy was more than capable of holding his own. He had wide cheeks and a bulb nose that cricked slightly to one side, the result of a bicycle accident as a child. Thick, dark caterpillar-like eyebrows touched over the bridge of his nose, and an inch-long scar, well faded over the years, was just barely visible over his right eye. He had the beginning of a double chin, and Ron figured that this was yet another law enforcement official that wasn't going to do anything to dispel the rampant rumors about cops and donuts.

"I mean, he was probably just a transient or something, you know," Pearson continued. "Somebody just passin' through. *Although....*" He paused and looked quickly around the field as if he might suddenly see someone, then looked back at Ron and continued. "We just don't get many transients up here."

"But we didn't hear a boat or anything," Janet offered.

"Not surprised. You're only two, maybe two and a half miles off the mainland. Somebody probably rowed out here thinkin' they might be able to pilfer something from the house. They prob'ly got all the way over and found out that somebody's in the lighthouse. They hightail it back to their boat and within an hour or two they're back at the State Street Bar and Grill in St. Ignace, suckin' on a Pabst and wolfin' down a burger." Pearson's voice was deep and throaty, and he spoke with a bit of an accent that Ron couldn't really describe. It wasn't southern or foreign, but had its own characteristics that seemed to be unique to the region of Michigan's upper peninsula.

"It was three o'clock in the morning," Ron stated with annoyance. "I can't believe someone would row out here that late."

"Happens all the time over on Mackinac Island," Pearson offered. "Somebody gets tanked up in St. Ignace or Mackinaw City and decides they just gotta go for last call at *Horn's* or the *Pink Pony* or somewhere. The ferries only run over to Mackinac Island till about nine or so. After that you're on your own, and some folks decide that a beer on the island would just taste better, so they row out by themselves. Not really the smartest creatures to represent the human race, but it happens. Well, no matter. I was able to get some good prints from the window. We'll find out who he is."

"And what about the blood?" Ron asked. The would-be intruder had pounded on the glass with his palm, leaving a perfect hand print on the otherwise unblemished window. Whoever was responsible had cut their hand on something as evident by the dark red stain that dripped from the print, running down the glass and seeping into the rotted wood of the sill.

"Well, there wasn't too much blood there, and I didn't see any more of it anywhere else around the house, so he probably cut himself somewhere on a branch or something. One thing I *will* do is check with the hospital to see if they've treated anybody with an injury of that sort. That might be a place to start, anyway. Now...tell me again what this guy looked like...." Ron and the Sheriff's Deputy were immersed in conversation, and Janet went over to the tent to talk to the Casey and Jon.

That is the weirdest thing, she thought. *Neither one of the kids saw anything, or heard anything...yet they both wake up screaming because of a 'feeling.'* The children said they had no idea why they awoke crying and screaming the night before, and for the most part had forgotten the whole episode this morning. Both wanted to go play, but Janet was hesitant, at least for the time being.

"Wait for a few minutes," she had told them. "Wait until Daddy is done talking." Jon and Casey didn't know what all the fuss was about and both felt very put-out over the fact that their morning exploring routine had to be put on hold.

"What if he's still here? On the island?" Ron asked the deputy.

"Well, he could be. Two hundred sixty-seven acres gives you a bit of room to roam. The island's about a mile long, maybe a half-mile wide. But if it's any help I'll spend some time and look around. There used to be an old town a little north of here. Little fishing town in the harbor. Just a couple hundred or so people. Nothin' there anymore, though. All the buildings have fallen down. No place for anybody to really hide...but I'll hike over and go check it out."

"Thanks," Ron offered. "I'd appreciate that."

"But I wouldn't worry. I think whoever it was is probably back on the mainland, long gone by now.

I hope you're right, Ron thought. *I hope you're right.* He watched the deputy as he strode across the field, into the woods and out of sight.

Ron looked back at the lighthouse and walked to the window of the parlor. The blood had dried on the glass, and he flaked some of it away with his thumb nail. After retrieving a rag he wiped away the rest of the ominous print until there was no more sign of any blood or smudges. He walked around the house again, inspecting the structure for any sign of forced entry, but found none. He passed the window with the wasps nest above it and walked in a large semi-circle, keeping his distance, peering curiously at the window and looking once again for the hand print that had been so defined in the glass just a day previous. Seeing nothing, he continued his search around the building, inspecting the door to the summer kitchen as well as the rest of the windows. Both he and the deputy had done so earlier, but Ron wanted to take a look again. Finding nothing, he finally forced himself to shrug it off and began the tedious task of removing junk and unusable timbers from the house.

Once again the day was sunny and warm. Jon and Casey were ordered to stay within the boundaries of the meadow, which seemed to be fine with both. There were logs to be turned over, frogs to be caught, and snakes to be chased. Ron and Janet spent the day removing mountains of debris from the old lighthouse. Old, rotting boards and falling plaster littered the floors in every room. Over the years the lighthouse had been a party destination for some, as evident by the many empty beer cans and old food wrappers strewn about. Someone had taken a cold black coal from a campfire and scribbled obscenities on the walls of one of the upstairs bedrooms. And most of the old furniture that had been left was broken and tossed about the weary home. It took most of the day to haul the debris out of the house.

"Hello up there!" The voice of the Deputy Pearson bellowed up to them from the field below. It was now early evening, and the sight of the uniformed man surprised them both. Earlier in the day after his brief search of the island proved unfruitful, he told Ron and Janet that he was returning to St. Ignace. He said he'd be back if he found anything out, but they certainly didn't expect him again that very same day.

Ron and Janet waved to him through a window from one of the upstairs bedrooms and carefully maneuvered down the old, crumbling staircase. The deputy met them at the front porch, and the two men shook hands.

"I guess I didn't expect you back so quick," Ron offered.

"Well, I really hadn't planned on it either. But we're supposed to get a storm tonight, and if the weather's nasty for a few days...well...I wouldn't be able to make it out till the waves die down."

"Find out anything?"

"Well, yes and no. Good news and bad news." The deputy removed a tattered manilla folder that he had been carrying beneath his arm. "The good news is, thanks to modern technology and computers, we were able to locate a perfect match for that hand print."

"And the bad news is you haven't caught him yet?" Janet mused.

The deputy drew a deep breath. His eyes shifted from Ron to Janet, back to Ron, and then down to the manilla folder spread open in his hands.

"The bad news is that he's been dead for fifty years."

CHAPTER THREE

"I don't like this at all."

Night had fallen, and Janet spoke uneasily as she stared blankly into the flickering light of the campfire. Jon and Casey were asleep in their tent, and Ron fumbled through a leather bag containing assorted tools and other hardware supplies. He put the bag back in the tent, checked on the kids sleeping in the small pup tent next to theirs, and returned to his wife's side by the fire. The wind had started to pick up, and the waves were beating heavier upon the shoreline only a few dozen feet away from their campsite. Miles out over Lake Michigan, a freighter blasted its deep, lonesome horn every few minutes. A storm could come up fast and furious over the Great Lakes, and now Ron wished that he had decided to bring the portable AM/FM radio after all. If a storm *was* coming, it sure would be nice to be able to get a local weather report and have an advance warning. He had wanted so badly just to shut off the world for a while and not have to think about wars and the economy and what lies were bouncing around Washington these days. But mostly he just wanted to escape the sobering reality of putting three relatives in the ground on the same day. Somewhere deep inside his anger still raged. But he would work it through, he told himself. He could work it through by just leaving the real world for a while. No phones, no TV, no radio...*no weather reports.* He hadn't thought about *that* while making plans to come to St. Helena Island.

"It was a mistake," Ron answered finally, stoking the fire with a stick. "That's all there is to it. Happens all the time. You can't trust computers for *everything,* you know. I mean...they don't even know who he is."

"Yeah, but...how can *that* be?"

"Easy. The computer found a match of the fingerprints from an old file...or what it processed as a match. But the file on the dead guy is so old that they don't have any information on him in the computer. No name, no nothing. I mean...It's obvious they made a mistake. Even Pearson himself said that. Except-"

Ron stopped himself in mid-sentence and was silent a moment. The Sheriff's Deputy *had* said that there was obviously a mistake...he just didn't know *how.* The best probability was that files were mixed up somewhere, meaning someone's prints got placed in someone else's file.

"But he said that's never happened before," Janet offered.

"No, he said that it *could* happen," Ron snapped back. His temper was becoming shorter as he was getting tired of speculating about possible solutions.

"Why do you think the deputy acted the way he did when he came back from walking around the island?" Janet wondered aloud, ignoring the anger in her husband's voice.

"How in the hell should I know, Jan?!?!" he exclaimed, reaching boiling point. "I mean...I wasn't walking around the damn island with him." The deputy had returned from his search of the island, told them that he had found nothing, and would be back in a few days if he learned anything new. He seemed nervous and edgy and had left quickly without any more conversation, but both Ron and Janet noticed something. The leather strap that secured his gun to his holster had been unsnapped, as if his gun were ready to be drawn. The deputy had caught them both looking at it and he too had glanced down, saw the flap unsnapped and quickly folded it back over the nine millimeter, securing the gun. His explanation was that it had caught on a branch in the swamp and he hadn't noticed the unsnapped holster until just then.

"You don't need to raise your voice," Janet said with a hint of her own annoyance. Lately Ron's mood was easily swayed when things weren't going his way, and even more so when things happened that were beyond the grasp of his control...such as a strange old man peering through a window and dashing off into the night. But she knew that there was much more to it than that. Ron had been devastated by the accident. He had become withdrawn and edgy since the funeral, often getting upset over even the littlest of things. Which, she felt, was understandable considering everything they'd gone through in the past few weeks. Ron drew in a deep breath and spoke.

"Well, I'll go take a look around the island tomorrow." His voice was apologetic, and he put his arm around his wife. He kissed her gently on her forehead.

"And leave me and the kids here?" she wondered aloud. It was less of a question and more of a statement, like a *you've got to be kidding, right?* type of response.

"We'll all go. Just tell the kids that we're going exploring. But I'm sure the deputy is right. Whoever he was, he's probably long gone by now. Besides...this place has been abandoned for so long that there's probably any number of people who venture out over the summer to hang out. It's not our island and we really don't have any right to tell anyone to leave."

"Yeah...unless of course they're pounding on windows in the middle of the night," Janet mused.

Dogs. A half dozen of them, yelping and howling, licking their chops, frolicking in anticipation. They stood together, mocking their prey, watching, waiting, like some half-crazed street gang set to kill an innocent bystander. They were ruthless and their eyes burned with hatred and fury. Casey's heart beat faster and she tried to run, but there was something holding her back. She was caught, caught in some web or net, and her legs spun frantically but she wasn't moving. She looked behind her and saw that indeed the dogs were now approaching, running towards her, their tongues lapping at their jowls. Their eyes glowed red, and Casey screamed as she kept trying to run, faster and faster, but it was too late. The leader of the pack leapt, flying through the air-

The loud thunderclap awoke her with a start, and she snapped over in her sleeping bag, tears streaming down her face. The horrible nightmare still glowed in her mind and her eyes swept the inside of the darkened tent, wary of the bending shadows.

"Jon?" she squeaked, her voice trembling. *"Jonny?"* Jon was still fast asleep. He'd always had the uncanny ability to sleep through anything. Or at least he was able to *pretend* that he could. This time, however, he *was* sleeping. A full day of playing in the field had worn him out, and not even the obstreperous clashes of thunder were going to wake him from his heavy slumber.

"Jonny? Are you awake?" Casey sat up in bed. The spring storm howled outside, and the wind shook the sides of the tent. Rain drummed at the canvas and the wind tugged at its sides, gently billowing the tent back and forth.

Misty shadows crawled up the sides, creating spiny black fingers that twisted and turned in the wind like bony hands that grasped at the darkness. Jon remained motionless, fast asleep.

Casey crawled over her sleeping bag and began to unzip the tent flap. It was very dark, but she could make out the outline of her parent's tent just a few feet away. Tiny raindrops speckled her face as she contemplated the quick run to the safety of her mother's sleeping bag. The dogs of her dream still haunted her mind and she peered into the darkness, expecting to see those terrible red eyes burning in the night, waiting for her to leave the tent, waiting for their opportunity to lunge at her.

A lightning bolt ripped across the night sky a few miles off, illuminating the field and the old lighthouse. Casey jumped, surprised at the sudden flash and its ensuing blast. But it was another light altogether that caught her attention.

Her eyes turned upward, toward the lighthouse not far away. Although the lightning flash had come and gone, a small flare now glared brilliantly in the sky. Casey looked up at the top of the lighthouse tower as the light grew in intensity and radiance. The entire field was aglow from the piercing white light perched atop the stone spire. A warm, comforting glow enveloped the field and the distant tree line as she looked on.

"Wow," Casey whispered aloud. She unzipped the flap more and glanced back at Jon. He lay quietly in his sleeping bag fast asleep, undisturbed by the raging storm that was engulfing the island. She turned again and looked up at the lighthouse, mesmerized.

The house began calling to her in the night, its soft whisper tickling at her ears.

Casey...Caaaaseeeeey...Come to meeee, Caseeeeey....

Casey stepped out of the tent and into the rain, her eyes intently focused on the shining light glowing from within the towers' lantern room. Suddenly she glanced around the field, still captive to the nightmarish vision of the pack of bloodthirsty wild dogs chasing her through her dreams. As if sensing her discomfort, the voice whispered to her again.

Yes...it's okay, Casey. They're gone. They've gone a long, long ways away. You'll be safe inside...Come...come to me, Casey...

She took a slow step forward, and the light grew brighter. She began to walk, very slowly, towards the lighthouse.

Come to meeee, Casey...Yesssss...come closer, child....

The wind and rain spun furiously about her as she waddled, almost tip-toeing, towards the dark lighthouse. Puddles of rain had formed but Casey was oblivious to them as she walked, eyes wide, towards the impending structure. She was now completely soaked and her drenched pink pajamas clung tightly to her damp skin. The wind howled through the trees, bending over branches and boughs in shadowy arcs. The billowing limbs were like giant arms, lurching, stretching, reaching over and down in expectation as Casey continued walking. She was cold and she shivered as a chill rocked her tiny body, but as she drew closer to the lighthouse, the air suddenly began to turn warmer. She stopped a dozen yards from the structure, her face glowing in the brilliant light. Her head was cocked back as she looked high into the night sky, gazing up at the dark shadow of the towering lighthouse. Rain drummed at her face and her hair stuck to her forehead and temple and clung to the side of her cheek. She blinked and wiped her eyes as she gazed upward.

Casey...Come, Casey...Come...in...siiiide....

Casey took another step forward, hypnotized by the glaring beacon above her.

"Who are you?" Casey asked aloud, still walking toward the house.

A friend, Casey. I am a friend...a very old friend. Would you like to play with me, Casey?

Casey continued walking slowly towards the voice, and now the lighthouse loomed menacingly over her. The glaring light atop the conical tower shined brightly as ever, sending jet-black shadows soaring over the meadow.

"Yes," she said finally. "But I can't see you." She stopped at the porch, staring up at the lit structure.

You must come inside, Casey. I am here...inside the house. It's warm in here, and dry. You do want to play, don't you...Casey?

Suddenly, a light sprang to life in an upstairs window. Immediately another window followed, then another, then another. Brilliant yellow squares opened up, flashing to life and illuminating the rooms within. Within seconds, all of the windows of the lighthouse glowed as if someone inside had turned a switch in every room.

Casey's eyes darted quickly from window to window. The house appeared warmer and more inviting. It was no longer the ominous dark structure that towered up within dark shadows. It was a haven, a refuge from the battering storm.

On the second floor, a shadow appeared. Casey turned her head up, raising her tiny hand to shield her eyes from the driving sheets of rain. The dark silhouette of a boy stood looking down at her from an upstairs bedroom. Rain streaked the windows and blurred the form, and the light atop the conical tower grew brighter still.

Come inside, Casey. Come inside and play with me. We'll have fun...I promise.

Casey took a step forward, lifting her foot up and stepping on to the porch. The house began to moan with pleasure, a quiet murmur that was lost somewhere in the roaring storm. It laughed and snickered silently to itself, waiting, beckoning....

Yes, Casey...just a little farther...just-

The lighting bolt shot out of the sky, a searing white streak that hurled from the depths of the storm. It leapt from the clouds, spinning, twirling and twisting as it blazed over the island, striking an old oak near the lighthouse. The tree exploded and enormous branches splintered and split away from the trunk. The concussion knocked Casey to the ground and sent her tumbling into the wet grass. Terrified, she jumped to her feet in an instant and began to run as fast as she could through the field. She tried to scream but no sound would come out. The rain beat at her face and she dove headfirst into the small pup tent, zipped the flap, and climbed frantically into her sleeping bag.

The shadow in the window disappeared. One by one the lights in the lighthouse blinked out, and the bright beacon at the top of the tower began to fade slowly, ever so slowly, until it was just a tiny spark, and then...vanished altogether.

The lighthouse was dark once again.

"How on earth did you manage to do this?" Janet asked as she stood over her daughter. Damp mud was caked over Casey's pajamas and on her arms and neck and her hair was still wet.

"I dunno...." Casey sheepishly replied, looking at the ground as she spoke.

"You're soaked and muddy and you don't *know,* sweetheart? Did you leave the tent last night?" There was a long pause as Casey sheepishly looked up at her mother for a moment, then hung her head and looked at the ground again.

"I dunno...." came the same shy, embarrassed response. Ron came out of the tent and looked at his daughter. Both he and Janet tried to get an answer, but they received the same response over and over again. Casey seemed quiet and distant, unsure and uncertain...not at all the happy, carefree child that was always the first to arise and awaken others, ready to attack the day and all it held for her. Ron started towards the campfire and Janet began fumbling through a nylon bag to find some clean clothes. Casey looked up, on the verge of tears.

"Dogs," she suddenly piped. "Lots of dogs. *Mean* dogs. They were chasing me and I couldn't get away. I couldn't get away from them and I was running and running and running and-" Now she *did* cry and she ran to the comfort of her mothers arms.

"It was only a nightmare, honey," Janet whispered, holding her tightly, comforting her. "It was all just a bad dream, sweetheart. It was just a bad dream." Casey pulled away and looked at her mother, determined to convince her that the dogs had been no dream.

"No," she said, shaking her head. "They were real. They were chasing me and I couldn't get away. They were mean and they had red eyes and they were going to hurt me. They were going to hurt all of us." She began to cry harder and Janet pulled her close and picked her up, holding her in her arms.

"No, sweetie. It was just a bad dream. It was all just a dream. Is that how you got all muddy? Running away from the dogs?"

Immediately Casey stopped crying and looked away. It was as if she were in a daze.

"Casey honey?" Casey didn't respond. She just stared blankly at the ground, gazing in to empty space. Finally, both Ron and Janet let the issue go. Whether she had been sleepwalking or if she had gotten up to go to the bathroom in the night and had fallen, they couldn't allow it to happen again. Especially if Casey herself couldn't remember or just simply refused to say. There was too much of a danger of her hurting herself or falling unseen and unheard into the lake. Ron and Janet decided that until they moved into the lighthouse, Casey would have to sleep with them in their tent.

Ron let the morning fire die out after breakfast. The storm had passed during the night but a light mist fell most of the morning and gray clouds suspended overhead like swirling balls of cotton candy, drifting slowly to the east. Janet walked the children to the lake and the three washed the dishes while Ron walked across the field to the lighthouse.

Funny how he always finds something to do when the dishes need to be done, she thought.

When she returned to the tents Ron was standing back from the lighthouse and waving her over with his arm. He had spotted something that he had wanted her to see, and his attention returned to whatever it was as she walked across the damp field and stood by his side. As she stopped he again raised his arm, pointing.

"I didn't hear a damned thing. Did you?" Ron spoke without taking his eyes off the enormous tree branch that had been impaled through the roof of the lighthouse. The huge oak limb was over a foot in diameter at its widest, and thirty feet long. The base of it had punctured the roof and was lodged firmly within the old trusses. Smaller, broken branches had snapped off and lay scattered over the roof and the ground. Janet squinted as she looked up, surveying the damage.

"Not me. I didn't hear a thing."

"Well, take a look at that tree. It's obvious it was hit by lightning. How could we be a hundred feet away and not hear it?"

Removing the branch from the roof took most of the morning. Casey and Jon played in the meadow while Ron and Janet used handsaws to first cut the branch into smaller pieces before carrying it off. Ron cut up some of the larger pieces to be used as firewood, piling it in a neat stack alongside the lighthouse. Every fifteen or twenty minutes Casey and Jon would bound across the field and run up to their father.

"Are we ready to go yet, Daddy?" they would ask. "You promised to take us exploring!" So far, all the children had seen of St. Helena Island was the lighthouse and the adjacent field. The prospect of being able to hike around and explore unknown territory was a thrill to both. Finally after Ron and Janet had cleaned the remains of the branch off the roof, it was announced that the exploration would begin immediately after lunch. Jon proclaimed that he was now a pirate searching for treasure, while Casey, struggling with an identity to associate herself with, in the end also settled for being a pirate. Ron said he would be Christopher Columbus, and Janet decided that she would be Joan of Arc. She finished filling a knapsack with sandwiches and snacks and handed the bag to Ron, who slipped it on his back.

"You want to take a couple cans of Coke?" she asked.

"Yeah. Stuff a couple in there. Oh...and grab those matches...you know...just in case. I don't think we'll be gone a long time...the island's not that big...but you never know."

An old path led away from the lighthouse and deep into the island. It was overgrown with brush and hard to discern in many places but Jon, who led the way by a few steps, didn't have too much difficulty in locating the main path. Cedar and spruce trees created a canopy over the trail, blocking the sky and darkening the forest. The swamp was very old and had never been harvested as evident by the numerous dead cedar trunks that lay decomposing on the ground. The air was damp and humid, and a few mosquitos and gnats buzzed about. In a few weeks when the warmer temperatures arrived the swamp would be infested with swarms of biting black flies, and it would be impossible to hike through the woods without wearing insect repellant. And even then many black flies were immune to the bug spray and if you weren't careful your neck and scalp would look like you had lost a fight with a vampire. In addition to the flies, Poison Ivy was prevalent all over the island of St. Helena, growing thick and in some areas filling entire fields. At this early month, however, most ivy shoots had yet to come up out of the ground. It wouldn't be until mid-June when Poison Ivy would begin to pose a threat.

Twenty minutes later the dense forest thinned, and the four found themselves at the edge of what once had been a small, thriving town. Only stone foundations remained. The skeletal frames of the buildings had long ago fallen away, the old wooden planks scattered haphazardly among the ruins. What once had been a small road weaved back and forth through the center of the forgotten town, overgrown with tall grass and weeds. Many of the old foundations had trees growing up through them, offering more evidence of how old the tiny village really was. Ron and Janet were careful to keep the children close by their sides, much to the dismay of both Jon and Casey.

"But Dad...how am I going to find treasure if I can't go look for it?" Jon protested loudly. Ron, for the most part, was searching for something else. He was looking for footprints, papers, wrappers, anything...*anything* that would indicate that someone had been here recently. They walked the entire grounds of the old town and found nothing that would indicate that anyone had been there. Or if they had, they'd done a good job of cleaning up after themselves. There weren't any footprints, no fresh wrappers...nothing to lead them to believe that there had been anyone around, at least not recently. Ron found some more old cans and a few beer bottles, but the labels were faded and bleached from months-if not *years*-in the sun.

The afternoon was wearing on, and both children were getting tired.

"Okay," Ron said finally. "Let's head on back," He was relieved, becoming more and more convinced that the old man or whoever it had been was long gone...certainly not on the island.

"Dad...can I *please* go look around?" Jon pleaded again. "Pirates need to explore. Please?" It wasn't necessarily *looking around* that he wanted to do...he just wanted to look around by *himself*...at least fifty feet away, where there was an opportunity to be able to find and claim something *himself*.

"Don't go too far away. Make sure we can see you."

Delighted, Jon sped forward, nearing the tree line and inspecting old foundations, poking his nose under rocks and logs and weathered planks.

"Where do you think he...*whoever* he was...went?" Janet asked as they backtracked through the old village.

"I think the deputy was right. I think the old guy left the island. There's no place for him to stay around here." They both took a look around the old foundations that were mostly hidden beneath trees and years of shrub growth and grass. If there had been any old buildings left standing, any structures to shield the wind and rain, then maybe...*maybe* someone could be hanging around. But there was certainly no place in the old remains of the village for anyone to find shelter.

"Well, there's always the lighthouse," Janet offered. "Maybe he wasn't very happy about us moving in to his home."

"It's possible but I just don't think so. There was too much old junk in there. If a transient or someone had been living in there it would have been more disturbed. Or at least we would have seen some type of evidence."

Ron carried Casey on his shoulders as they followed the path into the shade of the forest. Jon was ahead of the trio by a few hundred feet, searching along side the trail for anything that might be of interest. He kicked at stones, turned over logs, and searched the ground for anything that may have been left long ago by an island inhabitant.

A sudden noise in the bushes caught his attention, and he stopped. Even before he saw it, he knew what it was. He'd heard that sound many times before. The light *swish swish* that told him there was something small in the underbrush. He stretched his neck up and around, straining, looking....

The garter snake showed its head from beneath the grass, and Jon crept cautiously forward, his hands slowly extending.

"Come here, you...." he whispered. *"That's it...that's it...nice and slow...."*

The snake darted and Jon sprang. The thin black and yellow body struggled and slipped out of his hands, and Jon frantically tried to grab the snake again before it could get away. It slithered through a thick growth of saplings and Jon bounded through them, more determined than ever. His heart pounded wildly and his eyes darted madly about, scanning the ground, careful to look for even the tiniest movement. Although he had caught a number of snakes in his eight years, each one presented a new challenge and another thrill. He would always, he told himself, *always* catch snakes...even when he grew up.

But not this time. The snake had escaped. Jon looked up from the ground. His mouth opened slowly as he stared, unsure of just what he had found.

"Hey you guys!!" he called out. *"Over here! Over here! Look what I found!"* His excited shouts echoed through the forest and down the path. Ron, Janet and Casey were not far behind on the trail, and they finally brushed through the dense cedars to find Jon standing and pointing.

"What is it?" he asked his father. Ron set Casey down on the ground and walked over to where Jon was standing. Both Ron and Janet were silent.

"What is it?" Jon asked again, this time glancing up at his mother. Janet stood with her hands on her hips while Ron crouched down for a better look. Casey, uninterested, had taken a seat on the ground and was playing with a blade of grass with her fingers.

"It's a grave," she answered. Casey never took her eyes off her hands as she spoke, uttering the words nonchalantly as if she were bored with the discovery.

Both Ron and Janet, surprised that Casey would know such a thing, turned to look at her. Casey didn't even acknowledge their presence, her focus totally on the blade of grass in her hand. She truly could have cared less about what Jon had found.

It really didn't look like much of a grave at all. An old weathered picket fence in the shape of a box was nearing collapse. A huge cedar tree grew from within the grave site. It was enormous at its base, nearly two feet in diameter. The cedar overshadowed all the other trees, with a massive trunk that loomed up through the branches of the surrounding pines and spruces. Within the perimeter of the picket fence weeds and grass had taken over, growing wild and unkept for decades. The grave had quite obviously been there for a long, long time.

Both Ron and Janet crept closer, but Jon suspiciously kept his distance. Dead people, even if they *were* six feet in the ground, spooked him. He didn't even like going to cemeteries because he was afraid that walking on dead people would make them mad...even if they *were* dead. And with the funeral of his grandparents and uncle so fresh in his memory, the site of the old grave made him uncomfortable and nervous.

"How long do you think it's been here?" Janet asked quietly.

"Long time. Look at that tree. I mean...that's got to be a hundred years old or more."

The cedar tree towered above all the other trees in the swamp. In fact, the top of it wasn't even visible from where they stood beneath it. It seemed to rise high into the gray sky, up into the clouds, shrouding the top from view.

"It's not a very big grave," Jon finally said, gesturing

towards the pickets with his hand.

Ron looked around, looking for evidence of more grave sites. Janet did the same, peering around alders and trees and branches, but neither she nor Ron saw any.

"Why would someone place a grave way out here? All alone?" Ron wondered aloud. He knelt next to the grave and inspected the shabby fence. "I mean...there's nothing here...nothing that would indicate who it is or when they died." He looked for a small headstone or marker, but again found none. But there was no mistake that it sure enough was a grave.

"This is spooky," Jon quivered. "Let's get outta here."

Ron didn't hear him. His eyes were focused on a part of the fence, a part near the back of the grave. He spoke to his wife without looking at her, without blinking.

"Janet."

Janet drew closer, following his gaze to see what he was looking at. Her jaw dropped and she inhaled quickly, holding her breath. Ron got up and walked around the pickets to the other side of the grave.

"Can we go now?" Jon whined.

"Yeah, in a minute, hang on," Ron said absently. Right now he was too focused on the single picket that had caught his attention. He crouched low without touching the wood. Janet again approached his side and she too looked at the single picket in disbelief.

While all the other pieces of the fence were badly worn, some even broken, a single piece-one *single* picket-was nearly brand new. Its white paint literally shined in the daylight, in stark contrast to the other pieces of fence. But it hadn't been an old piece that had been re-painted; it was an actual *new* piece of wood...attached firmly to two very old pickets.

"How in the hell would somebody replace one picket without disturbing the others?" Ron asked.

"Why would they replace just one picket? That's what I want to know," Janet responded. Ron touched the new piece of wood, then ran his finger over an old picket.

"See? Look at this. It's brand new...but the ground is *undisturbed*. It looks like it's been in place for years. But that's impossible. The paint, the wood, even the nails...." His voice trailed off as he glanced at his wife. He could sense the terror in her eyes, could feel the tension in her body even before he looked at her. She was staring up at the cedar tree.

"Janet what's the-" he stopped in mid-sentence and slowly turned to follow her gaze. There, three feet above the ground, unmistakably...unquestioningly-

"Oh my God."

-was a bloody hand print. It was so distinct, so recognizable that it couldn't be anything but.

And it was *fresh*. The blood was still wet, and a tiny stream of blood was trickling over the papery, gray bark. The print was large, the size of an adult's hand. As they watched, the small trickle wandered in and out of the cracks in the bark. Both Ron and Janet stared in disbelief and shock. Ron turned his head and squinted between branches, expecting to see the shadow of the old man cowering somewhere from beneath the brush. He knew that he had to be around there, *somewhere,* smiling that evil, wicked grin, chuckling in arrogant pleasure at the prank. Only it was no longer fun and games, and never had been from the start.

"Let's go. Jon. Casey...Casey?!?!?!" Ron wheeled around.

But Casey was nowhere to be found.

Janet screamed and grabbed Jon by the hand. Ron bounded through the cedar trees and emerged on the path.

"Casey!! *Casey!!"* he called, running up the path.

"She can't be far!" Janet hollered, becoming more worried with every passing second. She picked up Jon and ran down the path with him in her arms.

"Casey!! Casey!!" she shrieked. *Oh my God,* she thought. *What if that...that man took her...what if-*

"Boo!" Casey leapt out from behind a tree, smiling from ear to ear. Janet jumped and Jon screamed. Janet set him down and whisked Casey up in her arms, too thankful to be angry with the childish trick. Tears streamed down her face as she hugged her daughter.

"Ron! Over here! She's okay!" Janet hollered, now beginning to calm down a little bit. Ron was there in an instant, running up the trail, out of breath. When he found out that she had been hiding from them, he was cross.

"Why did you *do that*?" he demanded, kneeling on the ground in front of her. Casey was silent.

"Why did you do that?!?" he asked again, raising his voice. Tears formed in her blue eyes and Ron stood up.

"Oh for Pete's sake," he said, shaking his head.

"Honey, she's a *little girl*," Janet scolded. "There was no harm done." She turned to Casey.

"Sweetheart...you can't do those things. Mommy and Daddy were *very* worried."

Ron stood a few feet away, looking back towards where the old grave was, and then looking up at the sky.

"Come on," he said. "Let's go back." He turned and started up he path, but it was Casey's voice that stopped him dead in his tracks.

"You know he doesn't like you, Daddy. He doesn't like you at all."

"She wouldn't tell me who," Janet said. "I have no idea." The children had long since been put to bed and Ron and Janet sat on two aluminum folding chairs, gazing in to the dwindling fire. They would all sleep in one tent, together. At least for tonight. Crickets and frogs echoed over the field in a repeat performance of last night, the night before that, and the night before that. The clouds were keeping the heat trapped low in the atmosphere and the night was warmer than it had been the previous nights. Deep within the island, the shrill whistling of a Whip-Poor-Will was faintly audible over the other sounds of the forest. The lighthouse was invisible in the darkness, as the stars and moon were hidden by a thick blanket of clouds. Ron poked at the fire with a stick and spoke.

"But what did she mean by *'he'?* Who's *'he'?"*

"I asked her, honey, but she said she didn't know. In fact, she denied that she even said it. I honestly think that she doesn't know."

"That's ridiculous. She's six, not two. And even if she *was* two, that would be no excuse. She wakes up soaking wet this morning and doesn't know how she got covered with mud. We'll be damned lucky if she doesn't catch pneumonia." Ron tossed another log on the fire and tiny orange sparks exploded upward, traveling with the heat, burning out before going more than nine or ten feet into the night sky.

"Do you think she saw the man the other night?" Janet asked.

"I don't know. I kind of doubt it. I mean...it was awfully dark. Did you ask Jon if he saw the hand print on the cedar?"

"No. But I don't think he saw it. He was on the other side of the tree. Plus he was a ways away from the grave. I'm sure he didn't see it."

"Not that it would matter much. But-"

"Ron...." Janet interrupted.

"Mmm."

"Let's leave. Let's just *leave.* I don't like this and I really don't have a good feeling about staying here. This place is starting to give me the creeps."

"Janet we signed a *contract.* We can't just *leave."*

"Yes, we can," she reasoned, her eyes pleading as she spoke. "Let's just pack up our stuff and-"

"And *what?* Tell Harry and the lighthouse people we

got scared off the island by an old man? Ghosts? Bloody hand prints?"

"Ron, something's not right here."

"You're damn right something's not right," he said, raising his voice. "Some old bastard is running around the island trying to scare the shit of us and make us look like idiots."

"Ron, I'm just-"

"We're *not* leaving," Ron interrupted defiantly. "We have a job to do and we're going to get it done." He had become angry at whoever was playing their silly games on the island. Someone, he was sure, was having some fun at the expense of his family. He wasn't about to give them the satisfaction of letting them know that he and his family were leaving the island.

"You don't need to get upset about it, Ron. I'm just concerned. For the kids sake...and for ours."

Ron, in a rare display of emotional control, apologized.

"I'm sorry. But all this bullshit...*whatever* it is...it'll be over...tomorrow. We just got here a couple days ago. Let's get settled in a bit, get the lighthouse cleaned up some more, and we'll be living in there in no time. Maybe even tomorrow night, if we can get the roof fixed. Things will settle down. You'll see."

Janet stared blankly into the fire. "I hope so," she said finally. "I *really* hope so."

Behind them in the night sky, the St. Helena Island lighthouse stood cold and alone in the gloomy darkness.

CHAPTER FOUR

Clouds and a cold breeze greeted the morning. Ron was up early, and he crept out of the tent to stoke up the coals and rekindle the fire. A flame soon appeared through the dry timber and he walked to the lake and filled up the stainless steel coffee pot.

Dark clouds billowed up from the west to blanket the sky and a fog bank was rolling in over the lake, still about two miles out. The temperature had finally dropped during the night and it was now much colder than it had been in the

the days previous, and Ron cursed himself once again for not bringing an AM/FM radio. A weather report now and then could be pretty handy, especially on a day like today. The mainland and the bridge as well as the other islands that were normally visible were now absent, cloaked in a gray mist that shrouded the water. Lake Michigan was unusually still and calm, and the subtle waves barely licked at the shoreline. A few seagulls huddled together along the beach, puffed up like little gray and white bowling balls to stay warm. They were oblivious to the man in blue jeans and untucked flannel shirt.

Janet and the Casey and Jon were still sleeping when he returned to the campsite. He placed the coffee pot on a makeshift grill over the fire and stood up, staring at the ominous gray clouds. It was a day just like this one, just a few short weeks ago, that he and Janet and the children had attended the funeral of his parents and his brother. The weather had been sunny from the day of the terrible accident all the way up to the burial...but that particular morning had been gloomy and dark and cold. Ron thought it strange that the weather could change so quickly from beautiful sunshine to dismal gray, dampening his spirit even more than it had been. Now the charcoal sky above the island took him back to that day, bringing back painful memories and final goodbyes. As his gaze shifted from the sky back to the ground he half expected to find himself still at the funeral, at the cemetery, to find that the time on St. Helena Island had been a fleeting moment in his mind and that he was standing by the three graves, still saying goodbye, still not wanting to let go, still torn and anguished and bitter. But when his eyes focused downward he was relieved to see the small campfire and the field and the distant tree line of the beginning of the swamp. The lighthouse sat dismal and desolate at the other end of the meadow, some hundred feet or so from where he stood.

The stories you could tell, he said to himself, shifting his thoughts. He didn't know all of the history surrounding the lighthouse, but he thought he remembered that it had been built in 1872 or 1873. The light had been a guide for ships as they navigated through the treacherous Straits of Mackinac, filled with dangerous rocks and shoals. During those years, shipping in the Great Lakes was booming with every kind of cargo imaginable. Lumber, fur, whiskey, iron ore, copper. The St. Helena Island lighthouse, and many others like it on the lakes, played an important role in the early days of shipping. For whatever reasons, the St. Helena light was only in operation until about the turn of the century before it was abandoned, left alone to fight the losing battle of slow decay and corrosion brought upon by time and the elements. The International Lighthouse Preservation Society had been formed in 1961 to help restore and preserve lighthouses not only in the Great Lakes, but around the world.

A red-shouldered hawk emerged over the tree line and screeched as it swiftly darted over the field, disappearing once again back in to the forest. Ron looked back at the lighthouse.

Now what's up with that? he thought.

The wind gently tossed his hair about as he squinted, staring across the meadow at the lighthouse.

The front door of the parlor was wide open.

Creak. Cre-eeaackk.

Ron walked warily over the front porch and approached the door. It was nearly all the way open, and he leaned to one side, peering in, then leaned and peered in the other side. He outstretched his arm and slowly pushed the door open farther. It gave a long, tired groan as it swung further, exposing more of the parlor. Ron took a step forward, cautiously inspecting the room, watching for a movement or some type of activity from within. The door had been closed last night, he was certain. And he was sure that the wind couldn't have blown it open, as it fit snugly into the frame. In addition, the wood had warped a little over the years, causing the door to close tightly. Ron usually would have to tug with a bit of force to get the door closed, and an abrupt shove with his shoulder would usually be enough to open it up.

He entered the parlor slowly, watching for any sign of movement. The floor cried out beneath his feet, squeaking in protest as he made his way down the hall, peering into each room, looking into closets. The summer kitchen was empty as well, and he turned and walked back towards the hall, gazing up at the staircase.

A noise.

It was faint, just a slight scuffling of something on wood, and it was coming from upstairs.

He's here, Ron thought. *That sonofabitch is here.*

It was impossible to walk quietly up the stairs. The old wood made too much creaking and rattling under his weight and it was pointless to try and ascend the staircase silently to surprise the intruder. He stormed noisily up the steps, looking up to the second floor, only glancing down occasionally to make sure he wasn't about to step on a rotted board.

Another noise. This time it was more of a scraping, a *scratching*...like fingernails on wood.

Ron was almost at the top of the stairs.

Suddenly a small, dark form charged forward, lunging straight towards him. Ron jumped and leapt out of the way as the big raccoon raced past him down the stairs. The animal reached the floor and never looked back, eyeing the open front door and making a bee line over the porch and out of sight.

Ron leaned against the wall of the stairs, shaking his head.

Damn thing, he thought, and managed a smile and even a lighthearted laugh. The raccoon had really caught him off guard and his heart was beating quickly, drumming within his chest. He took another two steps and was on the second floor.

The raccoon had scratched and scraped at the bottom of one of the bedroom doors with such fervor that tiny wood shavings lay on the floor beneath the door. Deep lines gouged the wood and Ron knelt down, looking carefully at the tiny pile of slivers from where the animal had clawed away at the door, pawing at the wood. Ron drew closer, looking at the bottom of the closed door.

The stench that drifted through the horizontal crack caused him to recoil, wincing. He jumped back and shook his head, feeling nauseous from the repugnant rankness. The smell had been overwhelming and almost toxic.

Shit. And Janet thinks my farts are bad.

He stepped closer to the door, carefully sniffing for a scent, hoping that it would be just a small whiff and not the powerful wall of odor that had nearly overtaken him when he knelt on the floor.

He could smell it now. It was a hideous, rancid odor that literally burned his nostrils. It was a putrid stench, not like a chemical odor, but more like the smell of something rotting and dead. Ron took a few steps back, inhaled a deep breath of clean air and stepped towards the door, grasping the knob. The door held fast for a moment before giving in and swinging open.

Nothing he had ever seen or heard could have prepared him for what was now before him in the bedroom. Ron rubbed his eyes in disbelief, expecting the scene before him to disappear.

The floor had become an ocean of blood, boiling and churning with the force of a storm at sea. Although the surface of blood appeared to be level with the floor it seemed to be much deeper, and Ron felt that if he fell in he would sink, sink to the dark depths of blood, however deep that may be.

And a *boy.*

He appeared to be young, maybe about Jon's age. His back was to Ron, and he was looking out the window. Blood licked at his black trousers, completely covering the boys' shoes. He was wearing a heavy wool jacket, and his brown hair was neatly combed. He just stood there, gazing out the window, oblivious to Ron and the tormented room of blood.

Ron couldn't believe his eyes. A bead of sweat trickled down his brow, down the side of his nose, and down his cheek...but he didn't notice it. His mouth was open and his eyes were wide in shock and disbelief.

The boy turned his head.

It was a gradual, casual turn, as if he had sensed Ron's presence. Then he slowly turned on his heels, facing Ron. He had full, round cheeks and a short, marble-shaped nose. And he was *smiling.* He was smiling, as if he had known Ron for a long, long time and was happy to see him again.

I'm glad you're here, Ron.

The boys' mouth didn't move, yet Ron was sure that he had spoken. He had *heard* a voice.

I said I'm glad that you're here, Ron. Aren't you even going to say hello?

Ron responded by opening his eyes even wider. He had heard the voice in his *head.* The boy hadn't moved his mouth or lips. He just kept smiling that same knowing, confident grin.

No matter, Ron. I can talk to you, and that'll be just fine. Do you know who I am, Ron?

The voice echoed through his brain and Ron looked at

the boy, trying to remember if he'd ever seen him before. He didn't look familiar at all. But there was something very strange about the boy's voice, and suddenly Ron realized what it was.

It was the voice of an *adult*.

It was a boy that stood before him, but the voice was much older, with the timber and resonance of someone in the later part of life. It was raspy and throaty, far too rich and full to be that of a child's voice.

I'm hurt that you don't know me, Ron. It makes me sad.

"I *don't* know you," Ron whispered slowly and quietly, shaking his head as he spoke. "I've never seen you before."

The boy began to move his head slowly up and down.

Oh yes. Yes you do, Ron. You know me. And you're going to get to know me better. Much better. In fact, we're going to be very good friends, Ron. You see, I have a job to do, and I need your help. I need you, Ron. His lips parted as his smile grew, looking more menacing and evil than ever.

"I don't know who you are!" Ron blurted out. *"I've never met you! Who are you?!?!?"*

The expression on the boys' face began to change, from a sinister smile to an evil, arrogant grimace. The boy looked angry.

"Who the hell are you?!?!?" Ron demanded again, louder and more forcefully this time.

And then Ron knew who the boy was. Suddenly, the face was no longer the boy's face but the face of Ron's father, bloodied and mangled from being thrown into the steering wheel. A hideous smile shined as blood dribbled down his nose and between his teeth. The boy raised his hand, gently gesturing towards Ron, coaxing him to come closer. The blood on the floor had now begun crawling out of the room, soaking Ron's shoes and seeping into his socks.

Again, the boy's face changed. Ron was now looking into the eyes of his mother. He could see her soft, gentle smile, her warm eyes gazing back at him. Only...it *wasn't* his mother. Ron knew it. It couldn't, wasn't, wouldn't....

Then Ron knew exactly who it was. It was the face of- *Death.*

Death, in all of its cruel, cold wickedness, was paying an unannounced, unwelcome visit. This was the unwanted guest that had showed up just a few weeks ago with three one way tickets. Death was there riding in the car on that terrible night, Death had followed the ambulances to the hospital. Death was the silent third party on the late night phone call from the police. Death presided over the funeral as the three were gently placed into the ground. Even then Ron was sure he could hear Death laughing, calling from unseen corners of the cemetery, watching, smiling, gloating in all of his arrogant, contemptuous power. Death had arrived, picked up his new permanent house guests and left, leaving sorrow and anger and confusion. Now Ron was facing Death again, in the form of a small boy, standing in a sea of dark red blood.

The face changed again and this time it was Death himself, undisguised. His features were grotesque and distorted, with an over exaggerated forehead and a freakish, long chin. A sinister forked tongue flickered about, licking his lips and wagging defiantly from side to side.

And the *laughter*. An evil chortle grew louder until it filled the room. It shook the walls and floor as the demon relished in the mockery. It knew Ron was powerless, knew that he was trapped, and it feasted on the sheer joy of it. The laughter became a choked, throaty growl as the creature's mouth opened wide, exposing sharp, yellowed teeth and a curling, blood-red tongue.

The figure took a step towards him and Ron backed away, bumping into the door frame. Suddenly the door sprang to life and flew at him, sweeping closed, fanning around with incredible force. It struck Ron and knocked him back, sending him tumbling over the railing and down the stairs.

Fuzzy images. Dark images. Confusion. Ron slowly opened his eyes, wondering why everything was so-

Dark.

In the next instant he knew. A board lay over his face. He was on his back, and when he moved his arm another board fell from his chest.

Then he remembered. He had fallen. No, he hadn't *fallen*...he had been-

He wasn't sure. As he sat up, debris began to fall away

from him. An old plank clunked to the floor as he carefully pushed himself upright. He rubbed his eyes with one hand and looked around. He was in the hall near the parlor at the bottom of the stairs. The crumbling staircase, already dilapidated and falling in on itself, was now almost totally destroyed. Broken boards lay strewn about the hall, some with nasty rotting nails protruding up from the sides. Ron's head ached, and he rubbed the nape of his neck with his hand.

Then he remembered the boy.

The memory made him stop, his hand still holding his neck. His head turned up, looking towards the second floor. For a moment Ron expected to see Death again, grinning that same, confident, evil grin.

But there was *nothing*. No one stood at the top of the stairs, and the entire house was serene and quiet. Outside, a few birds had begun singing, fluttering through the trees and dancing from limb to limb. Seagulls could be heard high overheard, spinning through the early morning sky. However long Ron had been out cold, it hadn't been too long.

Steadying himself on the wall as he stood, he felt around his head and neck, every few seconds glancing at his hands and fingertips in search of blood. He was relieved when he hadn't found any, and he felt better as he stood up. The fuzziness in his head began to fade and he looked around. Many of the steps of the staircase were broken, but it still looked solid enough to walk if he were careful. He took a cautious step up, gently placing his weight on to the first board, then another. The staircase moaned in pain as he did so, a mournful, haunting sound that cried out through the old lighthouse. Ron continued slowly, his eyes looking up towards the second floor, then glancing down at the steps, then back up again.

This is asinine, he thought, a wave of foolishness sweeping over him. At that moment he knew...he *knew*... that the whole thing had been dreamed up, that there was no boy, no blood, no-

Death.

As he reached the top of the stairs, the smell drifted around him again. There was a moment of apprehension, a moment where Ron thought that maybe, just *maybe....*

No. This is bullshit. All of it.

He took a deep breath, held it, turned confidently, and walked towards the room. He grasped the knob and thrust the door open.

There was no blood, no furniture, no evil demon staring back at him. The room looked like all of the other rooms: dirty and dusty, filthy from years of neglect.

There was only a hint of relief upon seeing the empty room. Ron knew that the bizarre images and visions hadn't been real, the face of his mother and father, the boy, of death itself...all were tricks that his mind had played on him after he fell. But the smell was definitely still there. He breathed in just a tiny bit and the putrid stench stung his nostrils. Ron stepped back from the room and closed the door, not seeing the tiny spot of blood on the floor as it seeped into the wood and vanished.

"And how long have you been hard at it this morning, Mr. Early Riser?" Janet asked as she stood in the doorway of the lighthouse wearing an old pair of very faded University of Michigan sweat pants and one of Ron's old flannels. She held a cup of coffee in each hand as Ron came out of one of the bedrooms with another armload of plaster. Over the years it had fallen off the walls and ceilings in chunks, and what hadn't fallen Ron had pulled off himself. It was all going to have to come down before they could even *begin* thinking about reparations.

"Pretty early, I'll say," he answered finally, giving Janet a kiss on the cheek as he passed her on the covered porch. He dropped the arm load of dusty plaster slabs in a pile that he'd begun earlier and joined Janet once again on the porch.

"Here. I brought you a fresh cup." Janet handed him a cup of coffee.

"Mmm, thanks. It oughtta be pretty thick by now, if that's from the same pot I started this morning.

"Yes, it's from the same pot...and yes, it's pretty thick," Janet replied, sipping from the mug in her hand. "Been pretty busy already, huh?"

"Got a lot done. What time is it?"

"Almost nine. Kids are still asleep. I think we wore them out yesterday."

"I think we wore out *me* yesterday."

"Me too. I think I-" Janet stopped talking and turned to look around before continuing. "Good grief, Ron. What on earth have you been *doing* here?"

Ron stared at Janet and then looked around the room.

"What do you mean?" he replied.

"This place...it's...it's *clean.* Or certainly *cleaner.* Did you do this all this morning?" Janet grasped her coffee mug with both hands and walked around, inspecting the floors and the walls. All of the littered debris had been removed, the floor had been meticulously swept, and even the old staircase, dilapidated as it was, looked much better.

"This is great, honey," she said, her eyes scanning the floors and ceiling. She carefully stepped over a small pile of old wood slabs and walked upstairs. The broken steps had been replaced by pieces of wood from the outside of the house. They were only temporary, but they were secure and would make the stairs functional until shipments of wood began to arrive from St. Ignace and Mackinaw City.

Janet stopped at the top of the stairs.

"Ron?" she called down. Ron took a few steps up the old staircase and stood by her. Janet was looking at one of the doors. She glanced at the door next to it and gestured with her coffee.

"Where did you-"

"I found them." Ron interrupted, already knowing what she was going to ask. "Back in the summer kitchen. I put them on this morning."

Janet leaned down to get a closer look. All four doors were old and worn, but now the remaining three doorknobs were brand new and shined like a new moon. Each one of the knobs had identical intricate designs and patterns woven in delicate curls and shapes. Janet stood back, then stepped forward to inspect another one.

"These other three doorknobs...are they new?"

"They were stored in an old box that I found in the summer kitchen." Ron repeated. "Probably never used before."

One of the doors was closed and Janet tried to turn the doorknob. It wouldn't budge.

"Locked," Ron said. "I locked it. The floor in that room isn't very solid," he lied. "And I don't want the kids in there until we've got some of those support beams replaced. Besides...we still have plenty of space. These three rooms will give us more than enough room."

"How about the stairs?"

"I think the stairs will be okay, but I'd rather that Casey and Jon stay off of them until we've gone up and down a few times to make sure they're solid. We sure as hell don't need'em falling' through."

Janet tried to turn the knob of the locked door again.

"Can I look and...." She turned to address Ron, but he had already turned and walked back down the stairs.

Jon and Casey awoke just before ten. Outfitted with jeans and sweatshirts and a *Detroit Lions* baseball cap for Jon, the two were off once again to begin their newly found rituals of bug hunting and frog chasing. For the most part, the children were good about not going near the water or venturing out of the meadow. Jon had caught a small grass snake that was the length of a pencil and he was keeping it in an empty Maxwell House coffee can, teasing Casey by threatening to feed her slug to his snake. Casey wasn't buying the taunt, being that her slug was half the length of the snake and four times as big around.

Later in the day the four ventured up the conical tower and the children got their first glimpse of what it was like to look out over the entire Straits region. Both children were dazzled, although cloud cover prevented them from seeing the entire mainland coast. Just a faint outline and the tips of the two tiers of the Mackinac Bridge was visible. Far to the south a few small pieces of land in the Beaver Island archipelago could be seen, but most of the other islands were obscured by misty clouds.

By late afternoon the sun had disappeared and the day had grown considerably darker, but so far the rain had held off. The fog bank still loomed over the water, creeping slowly toward the island. Ron again climbed the circular staircase up the lighthouse tower and looked off into the distance. Visibility had gotten poorer, and now the low clouds had obstructed any view of the Mackinac Bridge or Mackinaw City. Below him, Ron could see his children dashing through the field, and Janet was standing by the tents packing gear into bags. She had begun to move a few things into the lighthouse, and they planned to camp out on the living room floor while they worked on the structure. Sleeping on the hard wood floor would by no means be excessively comfortable, but at least the lighthouse would provide a bit more shelter than what the tents could provide. Especially if another severe storm was brewing, which is exactly what looked like was happening.

Ron looked down from his perch atop the lighthouse tower and gazed at the roof of the house.

Did I really do that? He wondered. The roof had been completely repaired. He had been so busy that he only had vague memories of being on the roof, repairing the hole from the big tree branch and re-shingling the damaged area. Only now, from his view from the top of the tower, he couldn't even tell where the hole in the roof had been. It looked as if *all* of the shingles had been replaced. In places where some of the shingles had been torn and ripped up, they were now perfectly uniform and aligned with a master's precision. He couldn't remember doing it, but he marveled at his work nonetheless. The whole day had been like that. It was as if it were a hazy blur, as if he wasn't really the one fixing the house but found himself merely a witness, a bystander, watching from a camera's view as the tedious job of restoration began to unfold. A number of times during the day he had caught himself working on a project without thinking about it, whether it was tearing out a floorboard or strengthening a support beam. Not that a task like that would be very difficult, but many times he had finished something and realized that he hadn't really *thought* about how to fix it. It was like he *knew* exactly what to do and how to do it without any forethought or hesitation. He hadn't sat back to make plans about this or that, but rather he had instinctively known what to do and in what order, how to go about it, and the easiest way to complete the task.

His gaze went from the roof, the outer walls, and back to the roof.

Almost like the damned thing fixed itself, he chuckled to himself. *No matter now,* he thought. *It's fixed, and that's the important part.* He climbed slowly back down the circular stone steps of the tower, closed the door, and locked it behind him.

Janet's arms were full and she carefully set the contents on the living room floor of the lighthouse.

"Looks like we've got our first decorations," she stated loudly. Ron was in the summer kitchen replacing some of the warped floorboards and he strode down the short hall and joined his wife in the room.

"What is it?" he asked, trying his best to sound interested. Decorations weren't really the first thing on his mind.

"I found these. In that old shed out back, in a wood box. The box fell apart in my hands, but these are still in good shape." She wiped away the thick film of dust and sediment on the glass picture frame.

"The lighthouse," Ron stated, matter-of-factly.

"Mm-hmm. From a long time ago. Look at this one." She handed him a dirty, ten-by-twelve picture. The frame was old and weathered and looked as if it had gotten wet over the years. The once dark wood was now a faded dirty gray. The picture beneath the glass was also damaged, but the image of the lighthouse and the tower was still remarkably clear. The dark shadow of a man stood at attention from atop the tower, as if looking out over the Straits, watching. The figure was too dark to make out any features, but it most certainly was a man, maybe with a cap. Ron couldn't tell.

"There's a bunch of old pictures, books, magazines... even some old newspaper articles," Janet offered. Ron seemed indifferent and set the picture back on the pile that Janet had set on the floor.

"I'm going to finish the-"

The two-way radio crackled and sputtered to life, and the distorted voice of Deputy Pearson filled the tiny speaker.

"Mackinaw County Sheriff's Department...this is the Mackinaw County Sheriff's Department...calling Ron Borders...Ron...you 'round there?"

Ron keyed the mic.

"Yeah, here. What's up?"

"Everything okay over there?"

"Sure. Shouldn't it be?"

"Well, I didn't know. We found your aluminum boat

washed up on the rocks northwest of here."

Ron paused.

"Our boat?" he replied.

"It's your boat. I'm sure of it. Have you checked to see if it's still there?"

"Well, I...well, *no*."

"Well it won't do you much good over here. Doesn't look like any damage has been done, other than a couple dings from bouncing off the rocks. But there's something else."

There was a long pause while the Deputy expected Ron to speak. When he didn't, the radio fluttered to life again.

"The line that tied it to the anchor was cut. Cut clean."

Another long pause.

"Somebody stole it?"

"Sure looks that way. They left the oars and the motor, though. Probably your old friend from the other night."

"So we don't have a boat."

"Well, not for the time being. At least until after this next storm rolls through. This is part of a system that started to move through the area the other day. Only this one is supposed to be worse. I can tow your boat back with the Waverunner but not until the lake calms down a bit. You gonna be okay in that tent?"

Ron keyed the mic again.

"Yeah, we'll be fine. We're not in the tents anymore. We're in the lighthouse."

Again, there was a long, awkward silence before the deputy spoke, the tension in his voice growing.

"You're where?"

"We're in the lighthouse. We got things fixed up a bit and we're here. There's still an awful lot of work to do. But we've got most of the major trouble spots in the roof fixed. Actually, the place is starting to look pretty good."

Deputy Pearson ended the conversation by telling Ron that if there was anything they needed they should call on the radio, but unless it was an emergency there was no way anyone would be able to get to them.

He sat back in his chair, staring absently at the radio. The Department hadn't been very busy, except that some idiot on a personal watercraft had gotten all tanked up earlier in the day and decided to make a run from Mackinac Island to Mackinaw City. The watercraft was found in the middle of the Straits beneath the bridge...minus its drunk rider. A few deputies were out diving for the body, but except for that single incident it had been a pretty quiet week.

But now he had something else on his mind.

He had never in a million years thought that Ron and his family would actually *move* into the lighthouse. He was certain that after a few days in the tents, wandering the island, checking things out...well, they would leave. They would leave like all the others had. Living alone on an uninhabited island may have its perks, particularly if you really wanted to get away. But the isolation was just too much for most people. Especially isolation on the island of St. Helena.

We're in the lighthouse. Ron's words echoed through Pearson's mind, storming down the corridors of his brain, gnawing at his head.

We're in the lighthouse.

He could see the Borders family on the island, smiling and happy, the children playing in the field. He saw them by the fire at night, talking, cooking over an open fire, laughing and telling stories.

We're in the lighthouse.

He wouldn't...*couldn't*... see them in the lighthouse.

Images hurled through his mind, horrifying, macabre memories and visions that twisted at his soul and crawled at his flesh.

Good God. They're in the lighthouse. They're actually in the lighthouse.

He stared at the thick manilla folder on his desk, its edges and corners tattered from use. It wasn't that this particular file itself had been used, but folders were not something that the Sheriff's Department routinely tossed away. A limited budget had to stretch as far as it possibly could.

He flipped open the file and absently thumbed through the inch-thick stack of papers, but he couldn't concentrate.

They're in the lighthouse.

He tucked the folder beneath his arm, stood up, and left the office.

Both Jon and Casey stood at the window, their noses pressed to the glass, watching the swaying trees. The wind rushed at the lighthouse and snarled at the window. It had grown dark early as the storm drew nearer, but still no rain had fallen. Janet was putting together sandwiches for dinner and Ron was finishing up repairing the floor in the summer kitchen.

"I'm glad we're not sleeping in the tent tonight," Jon said, his face still pressed against the window.

"You and me both, Jon," his mother answered. "You and me both. You two come and sit over here on the floor and eat. And for goodness' sake, Jon...put that snake in another room." Jon picked up the coffee can and looked through the milky white lid to see how his snake was faring. Satisfied, he carried the can into the foyer and set it down on the floor. Janet lit a half dozen candles and placed them around the room on a few makeshift chairs and a table that she and Ron had put together. It was only early evening, but the gathering storm had stolen the sun and six o'clock looked more like nine or ten.

"Ron...sandwiches are ready." Janet placed two peanut butter sandwiches on a paper plate and set it on the floor next to a napkin.

"Ron?"

No answer.

"Ron?" She strode down the hallway to the summer kitchen and turned the corner. Tools lay strewn about on the floor, and a hand saw in a miter box sat on a rickety table. She marveled at how quickly the summer kitchen was taking shape. The floorboards had been repaired and the floor was no longer warped and rolling, and the walls had been completely stripped of paint. Ron had fixed a cabinet and re-installed it on the south wall, and Janet opened one of the doors and found it already stocked with many of the pantry items they had brought from St. Ignace.

But Ron was nowhere in sight.

Probably out behind the bushes going to the bathroom, she thought.

The back door was open, and she stepped outside. The wind tugged at her blouse and pulled at her hair. She looked across the meadow and back along the tree line.

"Ron," she called out, cupping her hands around her mouth. *"Sandwiches...."*

No answer.

She stepped away from the lighthouse and looked around the other side. The tree tops were bent by the wind and the new spring leaves shuddered and quaked on their branches. A single raindrop fell on her forehead and trickled down her face. She wiped it away with her sleeve and brushed a lock of hair from her eyes as she continued gazing across the field. The meadow looked sullen and dark, and the young spring grass fluttered about in the wind. She looked down and saw her shadow and-

A shadow.

A shadow? she thought. *My shadow?* It was much too gray and dark and dreary for any shadows. Slowly, her eyes found the door of the tower. Her gaze wandered up the pillar, up, up-

-to the top.

The light in the lantern room was lit. It glowed brightly against the billowing dark clouds, capping off the tall white stone conical tower with a brilliant white radiance. Ron stood within the enclosed glass, staring out over the Straits. She called up to him.

"Ron!" she yelled. *"Ron!"* But he couldn't hear her. The loud, rushing wind shook the trees and drowned out her voice, and the fact that Ron was literally in a small glass room some fifty feet above her didn't help the matter.

"Ron!" she shouted one last time, waving her hands in the air. Ron still didn't hear her. He just continued looking out over the lake from within the enclosed glass room. The light shined brightly, and had she not been starting to get a bit irritated she may have appreciated its beauty a bit more.

She walked quickly to the door of the tower and turned the knob.

Locked? She thought. She pounded on the door and called again.

"Ron! Ron!!"

"What's the matter?"

The voice from behind made her jump and she snapped around. Ron was now standing in front of her, smiling. Janet's jaw dropped.

"How did you-" She stepped away from the huge tower

and looked up. The light shined bright, but the figure was gone. Ron glanced up at the light and spoke.

"I found some oil tucked away in the tower. Only about twenty gallons and it won't-"

"No...*no!* How did you get-" Again, she looked up at the glaring beacon. *"How did you get down here?"*

Ron wasn't sure what she meant. He had a puzzled look on his face, and his brow furrowed as he spoke.

"What do you mean?"

"You were just up in the tower. Not fifteen seconds ago."

"No...I was on the other side of the house. I thought I heard you yelling."

"Ron...I saw you at the top of the light. You were looking out over the lake."

"Honey...I lit the light a few minutes ago," Ron said, shaking his head. "I walked down to the lake to wash the grease and oil off my hands and I was coming to get you and the kids to see the light. See?" Ron held up his hands, still damp from the cold water.

"I saw someone in the tower, Ron." She glared at him, unblinking. The wind swished her hair about and swept a thick brown lock over her eyes. She raised her hand and pulled it away, continuing to stare at her husband. Ron took a step back and gazed up at the light.

"I don't see anything," he replied, shaking his head. But if it will make you feel better, I'll go check it out." His voice was placating and defiant, as if he were saying *I know you're wrong but I'll go prove it to you anyway.* He stepped around Janet to climb the stairs of the conical tower. Janet, indignant, crossed her arms and spoke.

"Don't you talk to me like that."

Ron stopped and turned to face her.

"Like what?"

"Like you don't believe me, that's what. You think I'm *lying?"*

"Janet, I'm sure you saw something...but it wasn't me. It was probably just a shadow or something. I'll go take a look."

He took the keys from his pocket and opened the tower door and climbed up the winding staircase. It was dark and damp, but he didn't have any problem finding his way. The air in the tower was stale and cold, and his heavy footsteps echoed within the tall brick cylinder. Finally he reached the top and looked around.

There was no one there.

Of course there's no one here, he told himself. He took a quick look out over the Straits, seeing nothing but dark cloud cover. Droplets of rain pattered the casing, streaking the glass and distorting his view. He climbed back down the stairs and closed the door to the conical tower. Janet was waiting for him.

"Well?" she asked, her hands on her hips.

"I didn't see anything," he answered, stuffing the key back into his pocket.

"I'm telling you I saw someone up there."

"Janet...there's no one else here but us. You heard the deputy on the radio. That old codger stole our boat and left. We're the only ones on the island." More rain began to fall, and Ron started towards the back door of the summer kitchen. Janet stood her ground, a few feet from the tower.

"One question, Sherlock Holmes," she sneered, her hands still at her hips. Ron stopped and turned around. Janet spoke again.

"If someone had to use our boat to get off the island, how did they get here in the first place?"

The spring 'northwester' as it was called battered the tiny island, trouncing the shores with eight-foot waves. The wind sailed through the trees and howled around the lighthouse. Eerie creaks and moans echoed throughout the house. Janet, Casey, and Jon were fast asleep on the floor snuggled next to their mother. Ron had lay down and tried to sleep, but after nearly an hour had gone by he sat up in the darkness and poured a shot of Yukon Jack into a new foam cup. He sipped the whiskey slowly, listening to the raging storm outside, feeling the strain of the old lighthouse with every whine and whimper of the ancient structure. The oil in the light in the tower had burned up long ago, and except for the occasional flashes of lighting the house and its surroundings were pitch black. Earlier he had been surprised not only to *find* the can of oil, but to find that it actually *burned* after all these years. It must have been sitting in the tower since it was abandoned. It took a number of matches and more than a few tries but the old liquid finally caught, and the light in the tower had burned very brightly while the oil held out. He decided he would make a recommendation to the Preservation Society to retain the light as an oil-burning facility. Originally, the plan was to automate the light through solar power...like most, if not all lighthouses had been converted to over the past few years. There were only a few lighthouses in the world that were still manned. Modern technology had eliminated the need for anyone to remain living at lighthouses, and the ones that *were* manned were for nostalgic purposes only. If he could convince Harry and the board members of the ILPS that a real, oil-burning light would have nostalgic value, they just may decide that it would need to stay manned full time.

And who better to man the lighthouse, he thought, *than the people responsible for its restoration?* He had thoughts of opening up the summer kitchen as a gift shop, of conducting tours of the lighthouse and trips around the island.

Heck...we could start our own ferry line, just like Mackinac Island. Mackinac lay on the other side of the huge suspension bridge. It was a prime tourist destination, and three ferry lines shuttled hundreds of people non-stop to and from the island throughout the day. The beautiful old homes and quaint harbor setting attracted people in droves for hiking, shopping, and sight-seeing.

Sure, he thought. *People would line the docks to come and see the old lighthouse and visit the island. And maybe the old town could be restored...just like it used to be. Of course that would take years...and a lot of manpower...but it could be done. It could-*

He paused in mid-thought and looked at his hands. His palms were sweating, and he set his whiskey on the floor and wiped his hands on the outside of his sleeping bag. Beside him, Casey squirmed in her sleep and snuggled closer to her mother. Ron's eyes had adjusted somewhat to the dark, and he could make out the three vague forms lying next to him in the dim room.

A bead of sweat trickled down his neck, and he wiped it away with his hand. It was actually quite cool in the house and he found it strange that he was sweating. He picked up the cup of Yukon Jack and returned to thoughts of tourists and ferry boats.

That's it, he thought. *Janet could give guided tours of the house. She's great at stuff like that. I could take people up the tower and show them the light. We could charge five bucks for the tour, not to mention five or ten bucks for the ferry boat ride. We could even-*

The lighting bolt ripped across the sky and a brilliant flash engulfed the room. Ron jumped and dropped the cup of whiskey in his lap.

"Ah, shit" he hissed. Janet and Casey and Jon slept through the thunderous explosion and he slowly got to his feet, cursing himself for being so clumsy. He had been sleeping in his old gray sweat pants and the spilled whiskey had soaked his crotch and most of his right thigh. He tip-toed into the summer kitchen and fumbled for a rag, finding an old ratty towel in the glowing light.

That'll do just fine, he thought, picking up the rag to

wipe himself off. He stopped.

The light? It was very faint, but it was becoming brighter by the moment. The lighting flash had long faded, but a glow remained, illuminating the area around the house and the meadow beyond. The driving rain hammered the ground and beat on the roof.

The light in the tower? he thought. *It's lit? It's lit again?*

He opened the back door of the summer kitchen and stepped outside, ignoring the driving rain and wind. The light was indeed lit, and now it shined brightly over the tiny island. Rain pounded the glass of the lantern room, and the wind roared through the trees.

There's no way in hell, he thought. *The oil burned out two hours ago.*

His bare feet squished through the grass as he walked away from the tower. From the doorway by the summer kitchen the tower was too tall for him to get a good look up at the light. Moving out into the yard would give him a better view of the lantern room atop the tower

The rain soaked his hair and drenched his sweats. It beat upon his bare back and shoulders, and a gust of wind sent a chill that shivered through his body. He stopped and turned back.

Rain filled his eyes and he wiped it away. The wind pushed it back again and he strained to see through the torrential downpour. His eyes burned from the heavy drops, causing him to squint and wince in pain, but there was no mistake. There was a man standing atop the tower, looking down at him.

Ron stood in the rain, his body rigid, staring up at the man in the tower. His anger boiled over and he drew a deep breath.

"YOU!!!" he bellowed. *"YOU!!!"* He bolted across the soaked grass, bounding through puddles and nearly tripping on a stump. The doorway of the tower was wide open and he thundered up the winding steps two at a time. His heart banged in his chest and his breathing was wild and forced. Up he went, around and around and around....

To the top.

Ron stood atop the lighthouse in the lantern room next to the light, shielded from the elements by the glass enclosure. He could hear his own heart above the storm and he snapped his head around, looking for the unknown intruder. He stepped outside of the light into the rain and ran around the small observation deck.

The man was gone.

"WHO ARE YOU?!?!?!" He screamed into the storm. *"WHO ARE YOU?!?! WHO IN THE HELL DO YOU-"*

He stopped.

The dark figure, holding a lit lantern, now stood at the edge of the yard below him. It was if he wanted to be seen, wanted to be caught. He just stood there patiently like a train conductor on a misty night, waiting to give the final boarding call.

"WHAT DO YOU WANT?!?!" Ron screamed again. The dark form slowly turned and began walking down the path at the edge of the meadow. His mind racing and his adrenaline raging, Ron exploded back down the steps, flying down the winding stairs and out the open tower door,

across the field and down the dark path that led deep into the island.

CHAPTER FIVE

Tom Pearson awoke around midnight, alone as usual, as he had been for the past three years. His wife Ellen had divorced him after her lengthy affair with some hot-shot attorney from Chicago who vacationed for the summer on Mackinac Island. Tom didn't get much out of the settlement besides a house payment and a 1988 Oldsmobile Cutlass Cierra that needed a new muffler. And a drinking problem, which was what he had expected after the night his wife had come home and told him she'd been sleeping

with Mr. Hot-Shot for some eight summers. He had no idea
who she had been sleeping with in the off season, but he
was certain that there had been others. The crazy thing was
that he had known for years...or at least he'd had his
suspicions.   There were more than a few out-of-town
weekend 'business seminars' and some very occasional late
nights 'at the office.' Tom wondered how she could have
kept up not only a marriage and a job, but an affair to boot.
And the way he had finally caught her was comical, like
something right out of one of those *True Romance* stories.
Ellen had done some stupid things before...but never *this*
stupid.   He'd been on patrol one night in St. Ignace
investigating a disturbance at the ferry docks. Nothing
major, just two men arguing about a small dent in a car
door and how it had gotten there. Ten minutes later the
matter was settled and the men left. But it was a car at the
far end of the parking lot that caught Pearson's attention.
The car was in the dark and away from the bright lights of
the dock, but even from where he was standing he could see
the car rocking back and forth.   Thinking that it was
probably just a couple teenagers, he snuck up on the car and
shined his light in the back window.

Surprise.

After the divorce was final he tried to eradicate his
emotional pain with the help of Southern Comfort, nearly
two-fifths a day for almost a year until he wrecked a patrol
car one night coming back from the *Laughing Horse Saloon*
in Hessel, a small village northeast of St. Ignace. Pearson
had spent a few hours there, watching a football game and
drinking with friends. He was off duty, but his Olds was in

the shop and he was driving a cruiser until the Cutlass was repaired. Tom left the patrol car parked at an angle around a curve on the highway so that when cars approached they thought it was a speed trap. The *Laughing Horse Saloon* was only a few minutes walk from the highway, and besides...Pearson thought it would just be better if no one spotted a Sheriff Deputy's vehicle parked in front of a bar for a few hours. After a number of drinks and a few shots to boot, Pearson had set off intending to return to St. Ignace. While taking a turn too fast the vehicle slipped on to the shoulder and Pearson over-corrected the car, sending it careening across the other lane and into a thick stand of pines. The car was totaled, and Pearson himself sustained a nasty gash over his right eye. It was pretty embarrassing for a Deputy Sheriff to wind up in that kind of trouble. He was suspended with pay until he completed an alcohol awareness class: ten one-hour sessions to be exact. If it were anybody else on the force, they probably would've been fired, but hell...it wasn't just *anybody.* It was Tom Pearson. Everybody had a soft spot for Tom, and what he'd gone through. If he'd been fired the community would've been in an uproar. Tom grew up in St. Ignace, as his father did and his father before him. The family name had earned respect over generations, and Tom himself was well liked and respected. He'd been with the Mackinaw County Sheriff's Department since he was twenty, was always willing to give those who deserved one a break, and he pretty much kept to himself. Tom volunteered to help out at church functions even though he had no particular affiliation. He bought oodles of candy and cookies and peanut brittle and God knows whatever else the local charity organizations were selling. He volunteered to be in the dunk tank at the county fair and during the Christmas season he dressed up as Santa Claus and rang the bell in front of the department store. Tom rarely, if ever, refused an opportunity to help anyone, even if he himself was the one who wound up on the proverbial short end of the stick now and then. After the accident most people felt pretty bad for Tom Pearson. The judge had decided a treatment program and probation would be enough, and Tom hadn't had a drink since...except, well, now and then he'd have a beer or two while watching the game at a friends' place.

But tonight he couldn't sleep. His thoughts and his dreams all centered around the Borders' family in the lighthouse. Pearson couldn't believe it when Ron told him that they had already moved into the house. He had honestly thought they would *leave*. Over a dozen attempts had been made to restore the lighthouse since that ILPS or whatever the hell it was had been formed in 1961. Most people had left St. Helena Island shortly after arriving, realizing that the job ahead of them was a task much greater and required far more work than what they had expected. The St. Helena lighthouse was in shambles...or worse. Tom wondered how it ever could be restored with its rotting timbers and worn foundations. Replaced, maybe. But not restored.

But then there were the people that *had* stayed...or at least *attempted* to stay. Pearson had even spoke to a few of them. Two years ago a man had remained on the island for nearly a month. Finally he wound up leaving in the middle of the night, rowing over to the mainland and flagging down a car. He went straight to the Sheriff's Department and told them what he'd seen on St. Helena Island. They pretty much just laughed, filed a report, and waved it off. But the local paper caught up with him and published his story. Jerry Hartmann was him name, and he talked about some of the weirdest stuff Tom had ever heard. Ghosts, noises in the lighthouse, all kinds of bizarre tales. Which certainly could be imagined, considering the history of the lighthouse. But for the most part it was just stuff you'd expect to hear about an old abandoned lighthouse. Pearson always thought that it'd make a good novel if somebody would ever spend the time to throw one together.

But that's all it would be. A book. A book of stories. A collection of strange coincidences, a twelve dollar and ninety-nine cent trade paperback filled with odd facts and fallacies and tales that some folks might or might not find interesting.

He reached over and clicked on the light beside the bed, listening to the wind howl and the rain drum the small wood porch attached to the back of his tiny house on Lake Michigan. He'd brought the manilla folder home and it sat on the table flipped open to an old article he was reading before he tried to go to sleep. It was a news clipping from 1968, about that crazy nut Fred Overmeyer. Another one of the few who *had* stayed to fix up the lighthouse. Or *tried* to stay anyway. This was years before the ILPS had gotten involved with St. Helena and Overmeyer had obtained a long-term lease and permission to restore the structure. His plan was to build a summer gift shop, which Tom thought was pretty idiotic anyway, since there was no way for tourists to get to the island unless they took their own boat.

It was *assumed* that Overmeyer butchered his brother and two workers that had hired in as help. At least they had *assumed* that was what happened. He had rowed from the island to the mainland in a small boat in the middle of the night, covered in blood, walking the two miles to the police station. The crazy fool claimed that the *house* killed everybody. Everybody except him. He was talking and babbling and rambling on like the madman he was, not making any sense. The following morning the police didn't find a thing at the lighthouse. Nothing. No blood, no corpses, no murder weapon, nothing. They were going to charge old Fred with murder, except they didn't have any bodies to prove anything. Sure enough, his brother and the two hired hands turned up missing, but damned if the police could find out what really happened to them. The state finally wound up shipping crazy Fred Overmeyer and his stories up to Portsmouth, which is where they sent all the loonies that they didn't know what to do with.

Pearson flipped the page and scanned another article. This one contained the story about a guy named Raymond Cooper. Same story, only this time three people were found dead in the house and Cooper was missing. He'd had a proverbial field day, hacking up everybody with a hatchet or something and leaving the mess for somebody else to clean up. At least they *thought* Cooper was the killer. No...they *assumed* it was him. They never found a murder weapon, and the bodies...or what was left of them...weren't discovered until some teenagers had traveled to the island later in the summer looking for a place to party. It was estimated that the victims had been dead for quite some time...at least a month and maybe more, judging by the way they'd smelled. It was *these* pictures, the actual police photos, that where the most disturbing. Ray Cooper had tortured all of his victims and chopped off their limbs, using the bloody pieces to spell out letters on the floor. What the letters meant no one knew. In one particularly grisly photo it looked like Cooper had written the word 'hi' on the floor...dotting the letter 'i' with a severed head from one of his ill-fated victims. Cooper was never found and although the case was still officially open, no new evidence had ever turned up. The grisly photos stayed with Tom for a long time, and even now just the vague memory brought upon a wave of nausea. Bottom line was that every time somebody tried to restore the St. Helena Island lighthouse, they either got spooked and left, or they stayed on. They stayed on until, of course, something bad happened. And it always did.

Pearson closed the folder and turned off the light, laying back in bed. Outside the storm battered the screen door like a whining dog scratching to be let in. Were it daylight, Tom would be able to see the tiny island of St. Helena through his bedroom window, just two miles off shore. During the day, he'd occasionally see giant Blue Herons fly across the span of water to seek refuge on the desolate, quiet island. During the day Pearson would see freighters far south of St. Helena as they navigated the hazardous waters around the Straits of Mackinac.

But at night the island was dark, and only on rare

occasions when there was a full moon could he see the black outline of the small, pancake-like shadow looming in Lake Michigan. No, at night, St. Helena was virtually invisible.

Except for tonight.

Pearson snapped up in bed, the cotton sheet falling off his chest and draping over his bulging stomach. He stared out the window, half in amazement, half in disbelief. He rubbed his eyes, expecting the vision to disappear, expecting it to be wiped away when he removed his hands from over his eyes. Rivers of rain pushed by the wind ran down the window, blurring the image. But the tiny yellow glow, way off in the distance through the sheets of rain, was unmistakable.

The light at the St. Helena lighthouse was lit.

In disbelief he crawled slowly out of bed, his eyes never leaving the tiny flicker in the distance. Warped streaks of rain coated the window pane and distorted the yellow flame, making it appear to be wavering back and forth. His bare feet padded slowly, silently towards the window.

"No, no, no, this is not good," he whispered. *"This is not good at all."* He stopped at the window and rubbed his eyes and glared back into the darkness through the storm. In the next instant the light vanished, as if some unseen hand had flicked a switch. Tom stood paralyzed, staring off into the distance for a long time. The last time he'd seen the light lit was-

Well, he didn't want to think about *that*. He'd refreshed his memory enough by dragging up Cooper's old file and flipping through it. He stared a moment longer before getting dressed and going into the garage to find his rain gear.

Ron cursed the darkness. It was a black like he'd never seen, and he walked with his arms in front of him, feeling his way along the trail. His face was scraped by sharp wet branches and overhanging limbs, making it impossible to run. He would have to go slow, swinging his arms out ahead of him to keep from bumping into anything more. The wind and rain continued to wail, but every so often he caught a faint flicker of light on the path some distance ahead. It would disappear for a few minutes, then it would appear again, only for an instant. Ron cautiously tried to pick up his own pace.

I'm gonna lose that son of a bitch if I don't get moving, he thought. He stumbled on a low branch and fell and his face plunged into the wet, syrupy mud. He got up quickly, wiped the dirt from his eyes and continued on, undeterred.

Where are you, you little bastard? Where in the-

Once again he caught a glimpse of the blinking lantern through the blinding rain.

There you are. We're gonna find out just what kind of game you're up to.

He could see the glowing lantern through the thick

branches and realized that he was gaining on the unseen man. Ron moved slowly, quietly moving limbs out of his way as he came closer and closer to the light.

One thick line of trees stood between he and the man. White light trickled through the dripping branches and Ron peered through the dense foliage, but the leaves and boughs were too thick to make anything out. Raindrops glistened on the spiny cedar leaves, and Ron's heart raced and his nostrils flared as he breathed.

All right. We're going to find out what this is all about.

In an instant he was through the cedars, lunging forward to attack his unknown foe. He thrust the wet branches aside and stumbled forward into the light of the lantern, ready for battle, ready for a fight, ready for anything-

Nothing.

The man was gone again. He had disappeared, just like he had done at the lighthouse tower. And the old, rusting lantern hung from a low branch of the enormous cedar tree, swaying gently in the wind, illuminating the bright white pickets below.

Ron's rage subsided and turned to disbelief as he stared at the pickets. All were brand new as if they had just been erected, and now they stood perfectly aligned and straight up, like a battalion of little white soldiers standing at attention. Brightly colored flowers were arranged neatly along the inside of the grave, and a small wood cross stood at the head of the site in front of the huge cedar. In front of the cross, a flat stone marker poked up from the now well-maintained grass. The shadow of the crucifix bent back and forth in the swaying light of the lantern.

Ron inched closer, his eyes focusing on the grave stone. Rain was running down his forehead and he wiped it away with a wet arm, ducking beneath a branch and stopping at the foot of the grave. The stone was slate gray and dripping wet, with an almost glossy appearance in the dim lantern light. He couldn't believe his eyes. The engraved letters on the stone seemed to be...*changing.* What looked to be names of people were appearing on the stone...names he'd never heard of. A name would arise and remain for just a moment or two. Then the letters would oddly twist and turn, reshaping themselves into another name.

Harrison....
Ridgemoore....
LeFlann....
Ellison....

Almost as quickly as he could read a name, the letters would begin to warp and distort and change and another name would form. Some were relatively common names; others were oddly foreign. Nearly a dozen names appeared while he watched. Half of him wanted to run, to turn and flee as fast as he could, but the other half told him that this wasn't happening, this *couldn't* be happening, that it was a dream from which he'd awaken from any moment now.

A strange feeling crept over him as if he were being watched. He turned and gazed into the shadows, around trees and branches, and realized for the first time that it had stopped raining. Even the breeze had died and the forest had become curiously silent, absent of the violent late spring storm that had been ravaging the island. He turned and looked back at the stone. It had changed again, only this time it was no longer gray. It was a deep, rich red, and as he watched the blood stain expanded, slowly covering the grass over the grave.

And the *name.*

It had changed...only this time, it had frozen.

Borders.

Ron blinked as if he had read the name wrong...but there it was again, chiseled in red stone, staring back at him.

Borders.

Horror rushed over him, filling his mind and engulfing his body. But he couldn't stop staring. The grave site was now completely red, covered with blood. The stain had begun to crawl up the white pickets, and-

Keraccckkk!

The lightning bolt violently tore open the sky. The brilliant flash was gone in an instant, and the lantern that hung on the branch flickered out. The wind picked up and the rain began again, and Ron was completely in the dark.

He spun on his heels, his mind in a frenzy. Branches snapped at his face as he fumbled in the darkness for the trail, the bizarre image of the grave stone burned into his mind. He waved his arms frantically in the darkness as he stepped forward, sweeping wet branches and limbs out of his way, then he stopped.

A light was coming towards him.

He froze, watching the tiny beam grow larger, hearing foot-steps sloshing closer. Suddenly, the light was shining in his face.

"Good grief, Ron...is that *you?* Ron?...it's me...Tom. Tom Pearson." The deputy shined the flashlight into his own face for a second so Ron could see. "What's goin' on? Where's Janet and the kids?"

"What the hell happened here?" Ron asked, ignoring the deputy's question. His face had a glazed over, sort of dazed look. Pearson had seen it before, in the faces of kids

strung out on angel dust or acid.

"Are you all right?" he asked.

Ron snapped out of his trance-like state and spoke.

"Yeah. I'm fine. I'm fine or I'm dead. One of the two. According to that grave over there, I'm dead. So you figure it out." Pearson shined the light through the dripping branches, sweeping the beam through the forest.

"Over there, I think," Ron guided. The pickets came in to view and the beam of light stopped. Deputy Pearson extended one arm and pulled the cedar branches away, stepping closer to the grave site.

"Now what in the-" Ron stopped in mid-sentence, his words left dangling in the air.

The old weathered pickets had returned. There was no stone, no flowers, no lantern, no blood...just the same worn pickets that had been there for years, and years, and years.

"I saw the light. I saw the light, and I saw it go out. That kind of spooked me, I guess. That's why I came." Deputy Pearson spoke quietly. "It was hell tryin' to make it over here. I had to come up from the north side where the waves were sheltered by the island. Took me over an hour in that old thing." He had motored over in his own wooden fishing boat. It was small, not an inch over twelve feet, and the tiny craft had been rocked and tossed about by the waves. As he approached the island the small dingy slammed into a rock, nearly puncturing the wood hull. He had beached it on the other side of the island at the old fishing village where there was somewhat of a natural harbor that provided some shelter from the howling west winds. Tom and Ron were now standing in the summer kitchen of the lighthouse, and Janet and Casey and Jon were still asleep in the parlor. It was early morning and the sun hadn't risen yet. The morning was quiet and damp and cold and a heavy mist still lingered, placing the finishing touches on the storm that had pounded the island only a few hours before. Ron told Pearson about the man in the lantern room and how he chased him through the woods, told him about the grave site and the small crucifix and the changing names. Deputy Pearson listened intently, nodding his head now and then, his eyes growing in amazement as Ron recalled the bizarre events. Pearson was even familiar with some of the names that Ron had seen appearing on the gravestone.

"That one...'LeFlann.' He was one of the keepers around 1910 or so."

"So you believe me?" Ron asked.

There was a long pause before the deputy answered.

"I'm not sure what to believe," he said finally, looking down at the floor.

Ron was quiet for a moment, watching the silhouette of the deputy's face in the darkness. Then he spoke.

"What's that supposed to mean? *'You're not sure what to believe'?"*

Pearson turned his head, staring out over the dark meadow. He told Ron all he could remember about the things that had happened on the island, about the rumors that the island was haunted, about Fred Overmeyer and Raymond Cooper and Jerry Hartmann and the people that were murdered. Ron listened intently, still drying himself off with an old towel. He had taken off his soaked sweats and left them in a pile in the corner of the kitchen and slipped into a pair of jeans.

"Well, I know what I saw. There was a man in the lantern room. I get to the top of the tower...he's gone...and then he's holding a lantern on the other side of the meadow. I chase him through the woods, he disappears and leaves the lantern hanging over a grave that's got flowers and shit all over the place. None of that crap was there before. It was just a tree with a-" He stopped and looked intently at Pearson. "You don't believe me, do you?"

Deputy Pearson paused, looking away. He turned back and faced Ron in the darkness and spoke.

"Ron...I dunno. I mean...I'm not what you'd call superstitious or anything, but then again, maybe I *am*. Maybe they're right."

"Maybe *who's* right?"

"Oh, there's quite a few stories that circulate over on the mainland and in Mackinaw City. About the first lighthouse keeper and his kids. Most specifically Virgil McClure, the keepers' son. I'm surprised you haven't heard any of this stuff."

"Sorry, but I'm not really up on my Straits Area Fairy Tales."

"And what a good one this is," Pearson chuckled. "See, McClure grew up in the lighthouse with his kid brother. Their father was the first keeper. His wife-Virgil's mother-died giving birth to Harmon...that's was Virgil's brother. Anyway, Harmon got sick or something...plague or flu or something like that. Died when he was six or so...'bout 1886. That's his grave out there."

Deputy Pearson paused, pointing towards the dark

forest. Ron nodded, and Pearson continued. "One day the old man comes back from fishin'...finds Virgil upstairs in his bedroom...with his *brother*. That son of a gun dug up his dead brother, carried him home and took him upstairs to play. Musta smelled worse than a road kill skunk. Been dead and buried for a month and ol' Virgil decides he missed him too much."

"Pretty sick kid."

"It gets better. Over the next few years, other kids on the island start disappearing. Vanishing. First there was like eight of'em all at once. Never found'em, nothing. They just disappeared. It was thought at first that they all must've took off in a boat and it capsized, killin'em all. But no bodies were ever found. Then, about every few months, another kid would disappear. Gone. Spooked the entire town. Everyone on the island wound up leaving by 1895. Everybody, course, cept' old man McClure and his kid. Oh, there were a few other keepers that stayed here at the lighthouse over the years, but the town itself was pretty much abandoned at the turn of the century. Anyway, a few years after most people left...oh, musta been around 1900 or so...somebody from town rowed out to deliver something. Found Virgil's old man dead in the lighthouse with a twelve-inch busted piece of glass stuck in his chest. They found Virgil out there...." Pearson gestured towards the forest again. "...sittin' in front of his brothers' grave. Looked like he'd been there for days with no food or water. And he had dug up a cedar sapling from the swamp and planted the damn thing right smack in the grave. Never gave no reason for it. In fact, he never spoke a word. Not then, or for the rest of his life. They sent him up to Portsmouth in the upper peninsula. That's where the state tosses all the nut cases. He died there in 1945. Was layin' on his bed, musta been about sixty. Hadn't spoke one word in forty years. Just before he dies he looks up and smiles at the nurse that had been takin' care of him for years, gets this wierd grin on his face and says *'gotta run...Harmon McClure's a comin' back.'* Nurse got so whacked out she went from employee to patient right then and there. In fact, a lot of folks believe that. Even today. Lots of people think that the ghost of Virgil McClure walks the island, waitin' for his brother Harmon to come back. Now I know it sounds crazy, but that's what lotsa people around here believe. They believe Virgil is some kind of lost, lonely soul...waitin' for his dead brother to join him on the island." Pearson stopped talking and looked at Ron.

"And that's it?"

"That's the story."

"So what does that have to do with what's going on now?" Ron asked, rather cynically. Ron wasn't sure he believed in ghosts or spooks or hauntings, yet he couldn't explain the things that had happened in the past few days.

"Maybe nothing. Maybe something." Deputy Pearson turned his head and looked away before he continued. *"All I know for sure is that those prints we lifted off your window definitely belong to Virgil McClure."*

A chill swept through Ron's body. He'd almost forgotten about the hand print on the window and now the vivid picture came back to him, the night Janet and he were in the lighthouse, the old man at the window, the bloody hand print, the boy in the bedroom and his macabre, twisted face. It was all too bizarre to even imagine. And now this....

"Are you sure?" Ron replied. "I mean...I thought you said-"

"There's no mistake," the deputy interrupted, shaking

his head. "They're McClure's all right. I guess I knew that the day I came out, but I didn't want to say anything at the time. You know. I mean...you didn't seem to know much about the island or much about what happened here. At the time if I woulda gone into the story you'da thought I was crazy myself.   Kids   disappearing...people   gettin' murdered...that's kinda too freaky for some people."

"That's a little freaky for *anybody,*" Ron interjected.

"Yeah, well. No matter. But I kinda figured that things weren't right out here. I just thought that you might get spooked away. Most people do. Funny thing is, most people around here take all these stories as the Gospel. Doctors, bankers...no matter. People with their heads screwed on straight. You think they'd be the last people in the world to believe in ghosts and spooks...yet ask'em about St. Helena Island. None of'em will even set *foot* here. It's kind of the bastard lighthouse of the Great Lakes, if you pardon the expression. Nobody visits here, you never hear much about the St. Helena Lighthouse in any books. Hell, there's a lot of people who live around here who've heard of the island and the stories, but wouldn't have the foggiest idea where the island is."

"And what about you?" Ron asked. "I mean...why are *you* here?"

The deputy paused and looked out the screened window of the summer kitchen, scanning the meadow. It was still sprinkling lightly and the dim gray of early dawn had arrived, giving the meadow a desolate, lonely appearance.

"Well, I guess I'm just a skeptic at heart no matter what. I hear all the stories, seen all the reports. I know something's going on, and it's really tough to believe in all the crap that you hear, but...." His voice trailed off. Ron quietly snuck back in to the parlor without disturbing Janet or the kids, and returned with a half-empty bottle of Yukon Jack and two cups.

"Whiskey?"

"Naw, I uh...ah what the hell. Just a little." Ron downed a shot and poured himself another, and Pearson sipped his slowly. They stood in silence for a few moments watching the dawn awaken around the small island. Finally, the deputy spoke.

"So, uh...what are you going to do?"

Ron swished the liquor around in his cup a few times, contemplating.

"Well, I'd like to say that this is all bunch of bullshit, which it is. Some way, somehow. But whatever's going on, I don't want to be involved. At least, I don't want *them* involved." Ron motioned towards the parlor at the other end of the house where his wife and children were sleeping. "We have to leave. Today. I mean...we've got a lot of gear here, but most of it can stay until I can make it back to pick it up later. But I want Janet and the kids gone today."

"My boat's not big enough to haul much except maybe one person," Pearson offered. "The patrol boat is a little bigger and I can bring it over...but probably not till some time this afternoon. It's in dry dock in St. Ignace getting some work done and I can make it over later today unless you want to leave earlier. Then I'll-"

"No, no," Ron interrupted, shaking his head as he spoke. "This afternoon will be fine. That'll give us time to pack up our gear." In the parlor Janet stirred, and Ron continued. "And explain to her. She had a bad feeling about this whole thing anyway. She'll probably be glad. The kids'll get over it. But they were starting to take a liking to this place."

Deputy Pearson said good-bye and told Ron he'd be

back at five o'clock that afternoon to pick up them up. He turned as he stepped out of the summer kitchen.

"And Ron?"

"Yeah?"

"Use the radio if you need to."

"Sure thing."

The deputy turned and Ron watched him walk across the meadow and disappear into the forest.

CHAPTER SIX

Ron looked up at the lighthouse from where he and Janet stood in the field. The rain had stopped, but the morning was dark and gray and quiet. The meadow was absent of the usual chatter and chirping of birds and other creatures, and not a single seagull winged overhead. Deputy Pearson said that all the weather reports indicated that more rain was on the way before the front was to move out late tomorrow. Ron told Janet all about his bizarre late-night adventure, about the man in the lantern room, the grave, the stone. Janet listened, her mouth wide open in disbelief.

"See?" she said. "I *wasn't* imagining things. I saw someone in the lighthouse too."

"Well, either way. I really don't want to leave, but I think it would be best. I don't want the kids freaked out about any of this stuff. Hell...*I* don't want to be freaked out by any of this stuff."

"What do you think is *really* going on?"

"I have no idea. I'd like to believe that somebody somewhere somehow is *trying* to make us leave the island for whatever reason. But I know what I saw last night, Janet. I mean...I *know* what I saw. The lantern, the grave, the blood. And it all disappeared, instantly, just like that. Gone."

Janet took a long look around the meadow and up at the tall, sweeping pines and cedars. In the dim gray of morning the island seemed so calm and serene. But the mellow surroundings had now taken on a darker turn...a turn that was all the more menacing because of the seeming innocence of it all.

"Where are we going to go tonight?"

"I think we'll just stay over in St. Ignace for a day or so. I mean...we really don't have a *home*. We'd planned on being *here* for a while."

They both looked up at the lighthouse. It had a calm, warm appeal in the gray cast of morning. It was hard to believe that so many bizarre things had happened here over the years. Janet focused her gaze on one particular area, one single upstairs bedroom window.

"Ron...why did you lock that bedroom door? I mean...there's nothing wrong with the floor or the support beams, are there?"

Ron followed her stare and now he too was focused on the bedroom window.

"No. I mean...yes and...*no.* The other morning there was a raccoon in the house. It had been scratching on that particular door upstairs. Anyway, I scared him off...when I opened the door, there was a smell in there that could choke a horse. I mean...it was *bad.* I fell through some broken floorboards and I figured it would just be best if we closed it off for the time being." It was only a tiny lie, if there were such a thing. Ron wasn't about to go into details about the grotesque visions of the boy and the blood, the sickening distorted faces of his mother and father, and the horrible face of Death himself. That would just scare Janet more, and besides...they were leaving. It wasn't important now. They wouldn't be spending another night in the lighthouse.

"What do you think the smell was?" Janet inquired.

"Well, I thought it was a dead animal. It sure stunk bad."

Janet turned to face Ron.

"What do you mean, *'you thought?'* You don't think it's a dead animal anymore?" Again, there was a moment of silence. Ron glanced back up at the window, half expecting to see the hideous figure, the contorted face of Death glaring down at him. Or maybe the dark image of the little boy, smiling and arrogant, taunting and leering at Ron.

I'm hurt that you don't know me, Ron. It makes me sad.

He glared at the window, seeing nothing except the

blurred images stored forever in his mind. That was the problem with remembering things. Too often, your brain was like a kitchen drawer filled with junk. When you took a good look inside, you never really knew what you might find.

"I don't know," he said finally. "But after what I saw last night, not much would surprise me anymore."

The clouds broke around eight a.m. and the sun played hide and seek with the large, billowing puffs of gray that floated overhead. The wind picked up and the clouds were once again moving to the east at a steady pace. A thick fog still blanketed Lake Michigan, cutting visibility to less than a hundred yards. An unseen freighter was navigating its way through the Straits as evident by the lonely sporadic blasts of a horn, lost somewhere within the fog. Jon had let his grass snake loose under his careful supervision and both he and Casey were playing with it in the meadow, and Ron had built a small campfire and was preparing a breakfast of oatmeal while Janet gathered together the things that they would need to take with them later in the day. They wouldn't be able to take all of their gear, and they wouldn't have a place to keep it if they did. Ron had stored their Ford Aerostar in a friends' garage just outside of St. Ignace, so at least they would have a vehicle, if not a home. They could stay in a motel for a few days before deciding what they would do and where they would go. There always seemed to be old houses that they could buy cheap and fix up as they went along, but finding the right one could take some time. And besides...although both he and Janet enjoyed working on the old homes, he didn't want to turn in to some home restoration gypsy that forever traveled from one dilapidation to the next, reincarnating homes that had died long ago. He was beginning to think that some of those homes were just better off dead. Either way, both he and Janet knew that bouncing from one home to the next every few years would sooner or later have to stop. It was fine ten years ago. But that was before Jon and Casey had come along, back when the weight of responsibility had been much lighter...more of a fleeting thought than a worldly reality.

"Hey you guys...breakfast." The children came running at Ron's call, Jon hastily scooping up his snake and stuffing it back in the can and running it back to the lighthouse.

"No you don't little mister," Janet scolded as Jon bounded back, sitting down to eat at the folding table beneath a large oak. "You go wash your hands. Both of you." Ron walked them down to the lake and in a moment they returned, both children with soaked shoes and grins from ear to ear. Janet just shook her head. There was some kind of natural law, some unwritten rule or something that if kids were near a lake their bodies just kind of absorbed water.

They all ate hungrily, and Janet gave the children the

task of washing the dishes and drying them off before packing them away. They would have one more meal in the afternoon, but that would be more sandwiches and snacks than anything. That way they could have everything packed and ready to go when Deputy Pearson arrived. Ron spent the afternoon picking up around the lighthouse, making sure his own personal tools had been accounted for. Things that belonged to the ILPS he would leave locked in the small shed. Throughout the day, his mind whirred with possible explanations that he would give to the Society for leaving the island so quickly.

Sorry, folks. Got scared by a dead guy. Yep, he's on the island waiting for his dead brother to show up.

He walked around the side of the summer kitchen and along the structure, taking a long, sweeping look at the building.

The roof was literally perfect. Old shingles had been replaced, and gone were the rolls and bumps caused by years of leakage. Ron had only vague memories of being on the roof, and certainly couldn't recall doing the work necessary to repair it to its current condition. Even the wood siding had taken on a new gleam. Many of the old boards that had lay strewn about had been used to re-side the lighthouse, yet the wood now looked in almost as good of shape as the day it were milled. Gone was the rot that had been so prevalent just forty-eight hours ago. It was if some unseen hand, some unknown force had aided in restoring the lighthouse.

And it was then that he *knew*. He *knew* there was no way possible that he and Janet could have restored the lighthouse to its present state. Not in just a few days. Hell, they couldn't have done this much work in a *month*.

He stopped in front of a window and stared. Just a few days ago he had seen wasps angrily buzzing over the glass... yet now they were completely gone. None buzzed about and there weren't even any that zipped in or out of the crack above the window. In fact, the small opening that led to the nest wasn't even there anymore. The wood siding was perfectly flush and there was no way a wasp or bee could squirm through. And yet, oddly enough, Ron was not at all that surprised.

He looked at his reflection in the window. His hair was tasseled and unkept, and his eyes were bloodshot from not enough rest. He hadn't shaved since before arriving on the island and a thick layer fuzzy of growth covered his neck and chin, along his cheeks, and up to his temple. The beard made him appear older and he stroked his chin, staring at the stubble. Much of his facial hair had gone almost completely gray, and on his head a few more silver strands had popped up just over his ears. There were weary bags beneath his eyes, forming dark semi-circles that drooped on each side of the bridge of his nose. His features were rugged and callous, and Ron found himself dismayed at how much different...how much *older*...he looked. He looked tired, like he hadn't slept much. Which, he reminded himself, he *hadn't*. He'd been up all night, first running through the swamp, and then talking with Pearson in the summer kitchen. It had indeed been a long night, and it was going to be a long day, too. He didn't imagine that he would be getting any sleep until tonight when they would check into a motel in St. Ignace.

A breeze rushed by and he squinted as he caught the reflection of Janet in the field behind him. She carried a burlap bag in one hand and placed it next to a growing pile near a large tree. Most of their supplies and equipment had been packed away and only the things that they absolutely needed would be taken back to the mainland, at least for now. Ron would come back in a day or so after the storm moved though and pick up whatever else belonged to them. Then they could decide what they would do and where they would go. Over the years he and Janet had managed to save up nearly one hundred thousand dollars, which was a fair amount of cash. But if they had to buy and furnish a home they could spend all of that and much more quite easily. Thankfully, they had a lot of options and certainly enough money to get by for a little while before making any concrete decisions.

He took another glance at himself in the window.

A hot shower, he thought. *And a Jacuzzi. That's all I need. I'll look ten years younger after a shower and a good night's sleep.*

He turned and walked across the meadow to help Janet with the last of their bags.

Pearson was tired when he finally returned home. He could feel the familiar tingling around his eyes, that ever so gentle twitch that told him that he hadn't had enough sleep. Now that he thought about it, he hadn't slept at all since the previous night. And he wasn't about to.

Not yet, anyway.

He turned on the small radio that sat on a cluttered bookshelf in the living room of his small cabin. Ellen had given him the unit years ago as a Christmas gift. It was a cheap radio, and the antennae had broken not two weeks after he'd received it. Ellen Pearson had never been known for her taste or knowledge of electrical equipment and had hastily picked up the gift from a department store on one of her many return trips from Chicago. She had watched Tom open the gift, nodding her head and blinking her eyes as if she were trying to encourage a favorable response. Tom of course said that it was just what he had wanted, and went on and on about how useful it would be. *Sure,* he had thought. *I'll be able to keep up on the latest tunes while you're getting laid 400 miles away by Mr. Hot-Shot. I get the hits and he gets the tits. Merry Christmas to you, too.* The very day after Christmas she was off again on some women's retreat or business expo or whatever the Excuse of the Month had been. There had been so many excuses that Tom had forgotten most of them.

A shame, he thought, as he adjusted the nob of the radio. *She had some good ones, too. Woulda been fun to save 'em and write a book sometime.* Being a Sheriff's Deputy, Tom had heard about every possible excuse imaginable. Not two weeks ago he had pulled over some guy from Epoufette, a small town about twenty-five miles northwest of St. Ignace. The man had claimed that *'I just couldn't have been speeding, sir, cause I always make it a point to go slow after I been drinking.'* And last year Pearson had snuck up on a poacher in a tree stand hunting deer out of season with a rifle. Two dead does lay at the bottom of the tree and when the man spotted Pearson approaching he had tossed the rifle as far as he could, shimmed down the tree and walked quickly towards the deputy. *'Somethin' wrong, officer?'* the man had asked, as straight-faced and innocent as they come. In his years of being in the department, Tom had thought that he had pretty much heard and seen it all.

Except, of course, when it came to St. Helena.

The radio buzzed and the broken fragments of a song crackled through the single speaker. It was supposed to be a shortwave radio as well as an AM/FM, but neither of the short wave channels had worked from day one. In addition, Tom had lost the AC adapter and had never bothered to pick up another one. He only listened to the radio in the mornings to catch the news and weather, so the four AA batteries that powered the unit would last about a year before needing to be replaced.

Steve Earle's *Copperhead Road* whined from the plastic grill as Tom emptied out yesterday's coffee grinds into the garbage and shuffled through a drawer for a new filter. It was a ritual that Pearson repeated endlessly over the past few years, like some kind of obscure robot programmed to do the same thing over and over, day after day. Open eyes...stumble to bathroom...piss...onward to kitchen...turn on radio...make coffee...sip from mug and contemplate upcoming daily routine. *Same shit, different day,* as the saying went.

The coffee maker gurgled and churned as Tom sat down at the small dining room table and looked out at the thick bank of fog that hung over the lake like a creamy white afghan that had been carelessly tossed aside, all crumpled and unkept. Once again it had taken him the over an hour to make it back to the mainland. At least the rain had finally stopped and the waves had calmed.

Tom turned back his sleeve and glanced at his watch. 9:08 am.

He pulled a thin blue directory from beneath the phone, flipping through the pages until he found the listing he was looking for.

The ring on the other end was more of an old clicking than the usual *biizzzzzzzzzzuup* that was normally heard by today's more modern phones. It was more like a series of tired clicks pressed together, a rapid repetitive drumbeat that sounded more like a dyslexic partridge drumming its wings than a high tech communications device.

Clulululululululululululuk.

Tom held the phone to his ear and tilted the mouthpiece to sip on his coffee.

Clulululululululululululuk.

Half way though the next ring the drumming stopped abruptly and a woman answered. Her voice was old and tired, the voice of a woman doing the same dull job for far too long for far too little pay. She had a drained tone that told Tom that she wouldn't be any more helpful than necessary, that he should be happy, if not *thrilled* that she had answered the phone, and he had better not ask for something that required the activation of more than a dozen or so brain cells.

"Portsmouth Wellness Facility. Joan." No *'This is Joan, how may I help you?'* or *'Joan speaking, how may I direct your call?'* It was a statement, not an offer to help. Her voice told Tom right away that she was being bothered, being taken away from more important work like watching *Jerry Springer* on the small TV below her desk.

And the name. Or, the *new* name, actually. *Portsmouth Wellness Facility.* Tom had never really been able to get used to that. Up until the mid-seventies the official name had been *Portsmouth Institution for the Criminally Insane.* Some politically correct dog-head had decided *that* name was too degrading for people who raped and murdered and killed people because the little voices in their head had insisted they do so. *'Institution for the Criminally Insane'* was far too negative...far too *assuming.* No, *Portsmouth Wellness Facility* was a much more dignified moniker for such misguided individuals.

"Uh...yes," Tom replied politely. "Dr. Posavic, please."

The woman responded simply by pressing a button and directing the line to another extension, for which Tom was grateful. He had no desire to even attempt to explain anything to Miss Boredom.

The phone buzzed once and was instantly picked up by an answering machine. A thick old voice with a slight Finnish accent began speaking.

"Hello...this is Dr. Emil Posavic. I am away from my

desk right now, but if you'd please leave a message I will return your call. If you have an emergency, press '1' to return to the operator...." The machine beeped and Tom began to speak.

"Emil...Tom Pearson here, St. Ignace. Listen...when you get a chance, could you give me a call? As soon as you can? I've got a couple questions about-"

There was a heavy clunk and then a loud squealing of feedback on the other end of the line. Posavic's gruff old voice bellowed through the wires.

"Tom? Tom *Pearson?*"

"Screenin' yer calls, huh Doc?"

"Naw. Just walked in the door. Hold on...let me shut this damn machine off. There. Lord, it's been a couple years. How are ya?"

"Fine, fine. You?"

"Older, wiser, and still kickin'." Emil chuckled as he spoke. It was a throaty, hearty laugh that echoed through the lines. "How's Ellen?"

"Couldn't give a rat's ass," Pearson answered. "Been divorced for a while now."

Posavic let out another good-natured chuckle. "Well, I'd say I was sorry, but it doesn't sound like you're all broke up over it, eh?" There was a richness in Emil's voice, a resonance of honesty and integrity. Old Posavic had to be well into his seventies, if not his early eighties. Emil told you how he felt, and if you didn't like it, well that was just too bad. At least you didn't have to worry about trying to figure out if the old man was just feeding you a line and telling you what he thought you wanted to hear.

Emil always laid it out straight, flat and on the table. He had lived in Michigan's upper peninsula all his life, and his father before him. Old Emil had even been a United States Representative at one time, and had been one of the earliest supporters of the movement for the upper peninsula to secede from Michigan and form its own independent state. It was a notion highly favored by most Yoopers, but cut down by political haggling nonetheless. Posavic served two terms and didn't run for a third but was re-elected on the write-in ballot anyway. He refused the office by resignation and the first runner-up took his place. Emil returned to his duties at Portsmouth, now no longer called an institution for the 'Criminally Insane', but a 'Wellness Facility' which was a term Emil himself scoffed at. *'When they come in here they're nuts,'* he had always said. *'And they ain't gonna get any wellness when they get here.'*

Pearson had been introduced to Emil Posavic years ago, as occasionally some escapee would threaten the pristine north wilderness and have to be rounded up by the authorities. The only way to get out of Michigan's upper peninsula was to either trek the two-hundred miles to the Wisconsin border, attempt to cross the International Bridge in to Canada (which was almost impossible) or to try and sneak through the Mackinac Bridge some one-hundred miles or so to the southeast. There were other ways, of course, but those ways usually involved a long hike through the dense woods or an even longer swim across a lake...neither of which were a very popular option. Invariably, it always seemed like Emil Posavic was the one who contacted the Sheriff's Departments and the Michigan

State Police Posts to give a full description of who they were looking for and what they were up against. Most fugitives were rounded up within a few days of their escape, cold, tired, hungry and confused. Pearson himself had his share of run-ins with escapees. Once an alert Mackinaw Bridge authority had noticed something more than a bit unusual. A man had paid the dollar-fifty to go across the bridge. Which wasn't all that strange except he drove fifty feet, jumped out of the car and stripped, shouted that the bridge was a god, and fell to his knees. He remained there, weeping hysterically until Pearson and his partner had showed up. The man didn't struggle or put up a fight as he was handcuffed. He just kept repeating over and over that the Mackinac Bridge was a god and that a terrible, terrible sin was being perpetrated by driving over it day after day. He made some nonsensical comparison of Jesus turning over the tables of the money changers in the Temple that was supposed to correlate to the toll booths collecting bridge fares. Nonetheless, Pearson remembered him as one of the most cooperative, polite people he had ever arrested, calling the deputies 'sir' and doing everything he was asked to do without question or complaint. Later he even apologized to Tom, saying that he hoped he wasn't keeping him from anything. It was the following day that Tom learned that the man had originally been sent to Portsmouth because he had brutally killed his family. Seems that he had thought his *house* was a god and it was immoral to go on living in it. When his wife had told him that they weren't moving, that it was their *home* and not some silly god, he had killed her as well as their two children by beating them with a fire extinguisher. He had stuffed their limp bodies in an old unused freezer in the garage and kept them there for weeks while he slept in a tent in the yard, fearful of the Almighty House God that spoke to him daily and gave him instructions to carry out. His neighbors said they had seen him praying to the home in the morning and when he came home from work at night. It wasn't until almost a month later before the bodies of his wife and two daughters were discovered by a suspicious relative.

"Look, Emil...I'm really sorry to bother you with this. But I need to find out more about someone that was a patient at Portsmouth a long time ago. But I think this was before you went to Washington. I think you know him." Tom paused, and when the silence was answered with more silence, he continued. "His name was Virgil McClure."

Tom said nothing more. His words hung in the wires, clogging the lines and suspending like low clouds on a rainy morning. Pearson waited, listening to the silence. He heard a sigh from the other end of the phone. Emil took a breath and spoke.

"Okay." His voice was calm...almost *too* calm, like Emil had known that sooner or later this time would arrive. Pearson had heard that identical tone dozens of other times when he'd have to call to deliver bad news to someone. Yet how could Posavic know that there was any bad news?

"Not on the phone," Pearson continued. "Not now. I'll be there by eleven." Tom didn't ask for permission, didn't ask if Posavic was busy, didn't excuse himself by saying that he didn't want to intrude. He would be there at eleven sharp...and that's all there was to it.

The waters of Lake Michigan looked over his left shoulder as Tom sped west along US-2. Portsmouth was only about ninety minutes from St. Ignace, but Tom found that he could usually make it in about an hour if he needed to. Unfortunately the huge deer population kept speeds at a minimum, which wasn't always that bad. Most travelers were forced to keep their speeds down because of the darting animals, and the aged, decaying carcasses on the shoulder and in the ditch every few miles were evidence that there were still those who felt the speed limit was a mere guideline and not a necessarily a law.

Portsmouth was a small town in the midwestern upper peninsula. In many ways, it was a lot like most towns that dotted through the heavily forested country. It seemed to appear from out of nowhere, this small community on a no-name highway north of Escanaba. There was a small sign that welcomed visitors to the town, two gas stations, a grocery store, a hardware and bait shop, three bars, (only two were open, as one had been destroyed by fire in 1990) and a small lumber mill just outside of town. There were only two things that separated Portsmouth from most small communities in the UP: a State Police Post that sat right smack dab in the center of town, and the large iron gates of the Portsmouth Wellness Facility. The police post had been added not long after the hospital had been built, shortly after one of the first escapees had killed a local resident before escaping off into the wilderness. But while the police post was highly visible to all who passed through, the Wellness Facility was much less discernable. There were no signs, no indication at all that there was any such facility in the area. A quick left hand turn just past the center of town led down a heavily shaded street that didn't look traveled much. The road ended abruptly after a quick right turn. Here, you had a choice of either turning around or proceeding through the twelve-foot iron gates. That is, of course, if you had business on the other side. Two armed security guards patrolled the fence, which was kept locked and manned twenty four hours a day, three hundred sixty five days a year. The iron fence continued around the perimeter of the property, each steel rod jutting into the sky and capped with sharp points that looked more like a row of carefully lined soldiers' bayonets. Above that, a two foot row of coiled razor wire spun along the fence like an enormous Slinky gone mad. A *dangerous* enormous Slinky that could slice skin like a paring knife and rip a person to shreds. Not many loonies got out of Portsmouth nowadays.

Tom stopped the patrol car and rolled the window down. The security guard checked for his name in the computer, finally nodding to Tom and waving to the other security guard to open the gate. The large iron bars swung slowly open under the watchful eyes of both men, and Tom waved and proceeded through. The gate closed behind him, and Pearson was alone on the grounds of what once had been the most infamous mental hospital in the state.

An immaculate blacktop driveway wound across a well-maintained lawn. There were only a few trees, huge monstrosities that looked to be hundreds of years old. At the end of the drive in the middle of the perfect green field sat the weathered gray stone building. Even as Tom approached he was reminded once again of an old prison, which, in essence, was what Portsmouth was. Or what it had been, anyway. In the early 1900's when it had been built, 'doctors' had tried to 'rehabilitate' their 'patients' through a variety of horrendous if not downright barbaric tactics and devices. Electric shock therapy was a popular tool and was considered a huge success for years, reducing human beings to zombie-like creatures that responded more like dogs than anything else. For rapists and those whose deviant sexual desires were considered unmanageable or out of control, castration without sterilization or anesthesia was common. This was considered a cure-all and was performed quite often on a number of patients in the early years of Portsmouth. It was cruel, yes, and drew much criticism and a bit of outrage even in *those* days...but one couldn't argue with the results.

But all of this was long ago, back to a past that only existed in history books and a few local historical museums. The Portsmouth Wellness Facility had been completely renovated at least twice, and now the interior did resemble more of a hospital than a prison. The floors and walls were a bright white, as were most of the rooms. Many patients were free to wander the halls, some chanting

to themselves in some language understood only by the
speaker.   Others just sat in chairs in one of the three
recreational rooms, staring blankly at the television set that
hung from a corner ceiling. The highly privileged patients,
the ones who had demonstrated that they were no longer a
threat to anyone, were occasionally allowed outside to
wander the grounds. There were even a few that had been
given jobs, tending flowers or shrubs around the old stone
building. Tom saw a couple people milling about, and they
saw Tom, too. They'd stop what they were doing and
watch the white patrol car pass by, wondering if someone
was being taken away or if someone was being brought in.
Maybe there would be another new kid on the block at the
Portsmouth Wellness Facility. Pearson glanced at their
sullen faces, wondering what this person might have done
and when they might have done it. Once a person was sent
to Portsmouth they never really left, and it was quite
possible that there were people incarcerated today that had
never left the grounds of the hospital in fifty years or more.

Pearson drove past the front of the building and around
to the side until he reached yet another iron fence. The gate
opened up and Tom drove into the staff parking lot which,
like the perimeter of the sprawling grounds, was completely
encompassed by long iron spears that were spaced four
inches apart. The lot was guarded as well, and an armed
security guard escorted all staff and visitors to and from
their cars. No car ever left Portsmouth without being
checked from beneath the hood and inside the trunk and all
points between.

The gate closed behind the patrol car and Tom parked

the vehicle. Instantly a security guard was at the door of the car.

'Mornin' Deputy Pearson." The uniformed man nodded as he spoke and Tom nodded back. The guard didn't know Tom, but had been radioed by the front gate to alert him of the deputy's arrival. "Dr. Posavic is expecting you." With that, he led Tom across the asphalt and through a set of locked doors, and then through another. This was the staff wing, completely off-limits to the patients of Portsmouth. Nonetheless, bars covered the windows and the entire atmosphere had a stale, cagey ambiance. Tom wondered how anyone would be able to work in such an environment, day after day, year after year like Emil Posavic had done for so long.

Pearson and the guard continued walking down a long corridor to an open door on the left. Posavic sat at his desk, a handful of papers in one hand and a glass of water in the other. His glasses dangled from the tip of his nose as his eyes scanned the papers. He looked up when he heard the two men arrive at the door.

"Son of a gun. You *did* come." The old man smiled as he spoke and stood up. The guard turned and walked away without saying anything more.

"You thought I wouldn't?" Tom responded smiling, walking into the office and extending his hand. Posavic came from around the desk and the two men shook hands. There was a kinship between the two men, a respect that each one had for the other. Emil's job was to keep people in, and Tom's job (on relatively infrequent occasions nowadays) was the undesired task of bringing them back when someone got out. And of course there were always those that were sent to Portsmouth for an 'evaluation' to find out if they were actually insane and unfit for trial for some crime or another. This required a police escort from wherever the accused had been lodged, and Dr. Posavic was usually the first person the new 'patient' would meet. He was a big, able-bodied man, youthful looking for his age and just as nimble as Tom had remembered him.

He gestured Pearson towards a big leather chair, then walked over and closed the office door. The two men went through the usual routine of *howyabeens* and *whaddyabeen uptos* for the better part of twenty minutes. Finally, the conversation turned to Virgil McClure.

"I must say," Emil began as he sat back down at his desk. "I hadn't heard that name in a while. Quite a long while, actually."

"Then you do remember him?" Pearson asked.

"Hell yes, hell yes," Emil nodded, raising his eyebrows as he spoke. "He was something else. I don't think he spoke one word the entire time he was here. In fact, I don't even remember him sneezing. Not one peep came from his mouth. Ever. Except of course, until the day he kicked off."

Pearson was disappointed. He had heard that old McClure hadn't said anything to anyone during his time at Portsmouth, but he was hoping that maybe it wasn't true, that maybe it was just a rumor fabricated by storytellers to embellish details about what would make a good ghost story.

"So he *did* die here?" Pearson asked. "I mean...here at

the hospital?"

"That's right," the old man replied. "Fact, I was here when it happened. When he died, that is. There was all kinds of screaming and hollering. Security officers came running in, the whole shit and kaboodle. Turns out that he was laying on his bed mindin' his own business when he turned to the nurse and said something about his brother coming back. And then he died, just like that."

"What did he die from?" Pearson asked.

Posavic thought about it for a moment and his eyes wandered up the wall like he had spotted a fly and was tracking its movement along the ceiling. Finally he responded.

"Don't know. I mean, I signed the death certificate. I just wrote down 'natural causes' for lack of anything else. He was in fine health. No heart problems, no illness. He got around well on his own. Kept to himself mostly. Spent his days in his room writing and drawing."

Pearson squinted in thought.

"Writing and drawing?" he inquired.

"Oh sure. That's another reason why we kept him here all those years. His drawings...and the things he wrote about his brother coming back. You could take one look at all that garbage he wrote and just know that he was a nut case. You might say that Virgil McClure was carryin' a full six pack...he just didn't have that little plastic thingamabob that holds'em all together. He sure could draw when he wanted to, though."

This was news to Pearson. Tom hadn't heard about Virgil actually writing things down.

"You mean, like..a journal or something?"

"Well, if you could call it that. It's more like volume after volume of warnings and premonitions and other mumbo jumbo. *Mostly* mumbo jumbo. Smoke?" Emil reached for a pack of cigarettes on the desk. "Not supposed to smoke in the building," he continued, placing the Marlboro to his lips and striking a match. "New state law. Screw'em." Posavic opened up a window as he lit the cigarette as Tom raised his palm, declining the offer.

"Volumes?" he replied.

"Hundreds and hundreds of pages. Maybe thousands. Most of it doesn't make much sense. McClure would write for a whole day and just run a bunch of words together that made no sense at all. I mean...*no sense at all.* Then he'd get on the 'Harmon McClure' trip and write about that for a week. All about how his brother was coming back. That, according to Virgil, would be the beginning of the end."

"The end of what?" Pearson asked.

"Who knows. Ol' Virgil was off his rocker the day he came in here, and he was off his rocker on the day he died."

"What were the pictures of?"

"Oh hell. I don't remember for sure. People. Some buildings, I think. Oh...and a lighthouse. A lot of drawings of a lighthouse."

"St. Helena?"

The old man's eye's lit up, and he blew a puff of smoke towards the window.

"Yeah. That's the one. Whatever lighthouse it was that he'd grown up in. He probably drew that thing a thousand times. Different angles, different colors. I'd try and make sense of them, but I couldn't figure them out. I guess we could take a look if you want to."

Tom froze. "Take a look? You mean...you still have the drawings?" He leaned forward in his chair in disbelief.

"Drawings hell. We got not only his drawings but everything he wrote. Locked up somewhere down in the basement. Least I think we still do. We got everybody else's shit...I'm sure we got his."

The 'basement' was nothing more than a very long corridor, twelve feet wide and God knew how long. It could have stretched on for miles. The air was damp and stale and reeked of rotting mildew. The floor was cement as were the walls, and the plaster ceilings were a dirty yellow and had obnoxious brown blotches creeping in from the corners, like the teeth of someone who had neglected proper oral hygiene for far too long. There were pipes that lined the ceiling that every so often crisscrossed and disappeared into a wall to serve their purpose somewhere within the old building. A few bare light bulbs hung from exposed dangling sockets like someone had hastily wired the fixtures on a budget and hadn't had enough money to finish the job correctly. Dirty, V-shaped streaks faded down the walls, offering more evidence of the clammy, dank conditions. There were spots on the floor that were obvious water stains from when the room flooded after a heavy rainstorm or during the spring thaw.

And filing cabinets. Rows upon rows of filing cabinets seemed to stretch along the walls forever. All were seated on wood pallets, each a few inches off the cement. As the two men walked down the narrow corridor the cabinets began to look older and older, like they had been placed in chronological order. Some were completely covered with a fine coating of rust from being in such damp conditions for so long. Emil carried a flashlight as the light bulbs in the basement were nearly forty feet apart, and in between shadows danced and darkened the cabinets. Posavic swept the beam over the front of the files, stopping every so often to mutter something about someone, most obviously a long gone former resident of the old facility.

"We keep all the old files down here. Any file that's more than five years old...we bring it down here. We really don't have any reason to come down here much. Most of these cabinets haven't even been *opened* since they were brought down here. Once in a while someone like yourself is tryin' to find out more about somebody...but usually the file isn't this old, and...*ah*. Here we are." Emil stopped at an old black filing cabinet that stood five feet high. It contained four drawers, most which looked to be so badly rusted that there didn't seem any way possible to open them. There were two entire filing cabinets...eight drawers in all that simply stated *'McClure; Virgil-deceased.'* The labels were handwritten on small cardboard labels that had at one time been white. They were now a dirty yellow-brown from too many years of cold humidity and darkness. The black ink had faded and ran, and as Tom looked at other labels he noticed that they too had succumbed to old age.

"Take your pick," Emil began. "If I recall, most are about the same. We could probably condense all of his garbage into two dozen pictures or so, and maybe fifty pages of his writing. But the damn state wants us to keep everything. I tell ya Tom...they're really startin' to be a royal pain in the ass. You're not gonna vote for that Clemsen guy for Governer, are ya? That sonofabitch'll screw things up even more than they already are."

"This is *everything* he wrote?" Pearson responded, politely deflecting Emil's political diatribe. "This is *all* of his drawings and writings?"

"Well, everything that we found. I know there was more, just because I'd caught him destroying a lot of it. Mostly he just left all of his papers on the floor in his room. Some of the stuff he packed under his mattress. Can you believe that? I've found every girly magazine imaginable between mattresses. I got one of the first issues of *Playboy* that was confiscated years ago. Worth almost a thousand bucks and its only got two pictures of hooters. Nothin' else. Anyway...the only thing that McClure saved between his sheets was his drawings and his writings. Take a look."

He tugged at a drawer. It held fast until Posavic gave it a heavier jerk. The file clunked open with a loud *ka-chug* and a row of manilla folders shifted for the first time in fifty years.

Dr. Posavic reached down and pulled out a folder at

random, bringing with it a musty, pungent odor. The folder had browned over the years and the edges were warped and bent but all in all not in that bad of shape. Certainly better than what Pearson had expected. Emil flipped the file open.

The first drawing immediately caught Pearson's attention. It was unmistakably the St. Helena lighthouse, drawn with such precision and realism that it first appeared to be not a drawing but a picture. McClure had used colored pencils, and the sketch was a literal work of art. The colors were blended perfectly and the lighthouse and the conical tower glistened beneath a beautiful blue sky. Even the trees were greatly detailed right down to each individual leaf and needle. Tom raised the picture up and stared, admiring the work. The paper, like the manilla folder, was yellowed with age and the edges were curling in. The thin sheets had grown brittle and rigid over the years, crackling and creaking like the bones of an old, old man.

"There's more in here-" Posavic tugged at another drawer, succeeding in pulling it out a few inches. "And here." He pointed to yet another cabinet and his brow furrowed as he spoke. Thick ripples formed on his forehead creating dark, horizontal bars. "Old McClure was a little more creative than most of our-" Dr. Posavic's voice was interrupted by a shrill beeping. He grabbed at his waist and snapped the pager from his belt.

"Whoop. Looks like I gotta run for a few minutes." He held the pager up, squinting as he pulled it closer. "Four thirty-three. That's William Allerman's room. Probably attacking the television again." He handed the flashlight to Pearson. "Sorry the light's not real good down here. Stay as long as you want, just shut the lights off when you come up. I'll let security know that you're down here."

Emil turned and walked away, but Pearson hardly noticed and didn't say a word. He was too focused on the drawing, too amazed at the intricate artwork of Virgil McClure. Tom barely heard the footsteps echoing away, plodding slowly up the old cement steps, finally fading out altogether.

He was alone.

The fog bank that had covered Lake Michigan was stubborn and belligerent, refusing to budge and settling instead to just shift around to protect its territory, finally drifting north around noon to devour the entire island. The air turned colder and billowing wisps of wet fog fingered slowly over the island of St. Helena, slithering in and around the lighthouse and the conical tower like thousands of thick white fingers.

Ron climbed the circular steps to the lantern room but the fog was so thick that it was impossible to see anything. The big lake below him, the islands towards the southwest, the bridge...all had vanished in the impenetrable gray mist.

Even the trees and ground only a few dozen yards below were clouded and difficult to discern. Casey and Jon were playing near the porch of the lighthouse, and he could barely make out their dark silhouettes through the fog. Janet was still preparing the items they would be taking back to the mainland and had just finished packing a bag and placed it near the front door. Ron thought about lighting the oil in the light, giving any ships in the Straits something to guide by, but decided against it. He was certain there wouldn't be any ships navigating the waters in *these* conditions. And with the good potential of a fierce storm tonight, he figured that most ships would just stay hunkered down for the next day or so, safe in port. He gave one last look around the small room in the conical tower, turned, walked back down the spiraling stairs, and locked the door behind him. Then, remembering that he'd need to get a few things out of the tower before they left that evening, he unlocked the door and opened it just a crack. He looked up into the mist, up at the tower and above the house. A milky-white haze draped over the meadow and obscured the trees. It was cold and clammy on his skin and he rubbed his arms, wiping away the slippery dampness.

"Ron?" Janet called out from the front door of the lighthouse. "Come here and look at this." She disappeared and Ron walked towards the porch. Jon and Casey sat cross-legged in the grass, each with a watchful eye on their respective pets. Every few seconds when his snake would be in danger of escaping Jon would pick it up by the tail and bring it closer once again. Casey's slug was virtually comatose, frozen to a large green leaf that she held in her hands. Ron walked across the porch and into the house.

Janet sat on a wooden crate at one of the make-shift tables. An old cardboard box sat at her feet, and a pile of papers was spread out before her. She held an old clipping in her hands.

"What's up?" he asked, standing beside her. Janet handed him the news article. The paper was faded and old and smelled of rank mildew.

"Take a look at this. These clippings are things that have happened here on St. Helena over the years. Some of these articles date back to the late eighteen-hundreds."

Ron held the newspaper clipping in his hand. The story was from long ago when Beaver Island, a large island to the southwest, contained a colony of Mormons. Their leader, King Strang, had been assassinated. The story detailed the events of how some of the early residents of St. Helena pillaged Beaver Island and virtually 'evicted' the remaining Mormons. After taking what they wanted the men retreated to the small village on the island of St. Helena. Unfortunately for the Mormons, they weren't in the grace of favor of any courts or law enforcement agency, and no charges were ever filed in the ransacking.

But there were other news clippings with a decidedly different twist. Stories about some of the goings-on at the lighthouse on St. Helena. Some of the stories confirmed what Deputy Pearson had told Ron earlier. Missing boys, Virgil McClure's bizarre behavior...even the behavior of subsequent lighthouse keepers. One lengthy clipping was that of a man who claimed to have seen strange ships navigating the Straits during the night. Most were ships that had been reported missing or lost for a number of years, and the man went on to describe in great detail how the ships sailed through the night and early morning hours. The story was more of a feature-type human interest story, kind of like an early day *National Enquirer.*

But one particularly nauseating account related the grim story of a lighthouse keeper that had been mauled and eaten by his own dogs. Apparently the keeper had died of a heart attack and, without a hand to feed them, the animals were forced to fend for their own meals. The keeper's well-eaten remains were discovered by a friend from St. Ignace who hadn't heard from the man in a while. The hungry dogs had reduced the man to not much more than bones and torn clothing. All in all, seven dogs were found roaming the island in a pack, taking down deer and other animals. All had to be shot and killed.

"Some of this stuff is just too weird," Janet said, not taking her eyes off the old clipping. "If I knew about this before I'm not sure if I'd be here now. I think-" Janet was interrupted by a scraping noise from the summer kitchen. It was a distinct scratching, like a scrape of nails on wood. Like-

Ron walked down the hall and towards the sound.

...like a paw scratching at the door.

"I think our little raccoon friend is paying us a visit," he said, handing the clipping back to Janet. He strode into the summer kitchen and the methodic scratching stopped, followed by the pattering of something darting off, like a child might ring a doorbell and run away.

Ron opened the door.

A dog ran across the yard, speeding over the grass. Then, just as the animal looked as if were about to vanish in the mist it slowed, glancing back with leering, hateful eyes and a rolling, frolicking tongue. The dog turned around and stopped. It was dark colored and mangy, and its fur clung together in mats. It looked as if it may have been a German Shepard, but it was so skinny and ragged that Ron couldn't tell. It stood in the distance, barely visibly through the gray fog.

Another dog appeared, slowly joining the other animal. Then another sauntered up, standing a few feet from the other two. This dog was obviously a Doberman, with dirty black fur and jet-black eyes. It lowered its head as it stopped, staring straight ahead, watching. It was joined by another, then another. Soon, seven dogs stood together in arrogant defiance, their mouths open and tongues hanging. They were all about the same size except for one enormous dog that stood off to the side of the others. It too was filthy, but the multi-colored markings of a husky were visible even from a distance. The dog had one blue eye and one black eye, only adding to its wicked, sinister demeanor. The animals remained perfectly still, staring back at Ron and Janet in the doorway.

"Ron...what is going on here?!?" Janet whispered. Ron was silent. *"We were just reading about-"* she stopped talking as she snapped her head around to look back at the pile of newspapers and clippings on the floor at the other end of the hall. In the yard, the dogs remained frozen and unmoving, as if daring the two to step out of the summer kitchen. Seconds passed and the dogs showed no signs of

movement, except for the subtle bobbing of their heads as they panted, their mouths still wide, tongues lolling to the sides of their jowls.

"*Git!*" Ron yelled suddenly. His voice echoed over the field and faded quickly in the dense mist. The dogs showed no response, no motion. Not even an acknowledgment of being addressed. The line of dogs just stood there, and Ron wasn't sure if they were watching him or ignoring him.

No, they're watching me all right, he thought, taking a step down from the doorway of the summer kitchen. As he did so a couple of the dogs lowered their heads and poised as if they were ready to lunge. Ron picked up a stick and threw it at them. It fell a few feet in front of the pack but they continued to stand motionless as if they hadn't even seen the limb hit the ground. Ron took a step back into the summer kitchen.

Suddenly, a shrill cry echoed over the meadow.

"*Jonny! Stop it!! You're gonna squish him!!*"

It was Casey.

Now the dogs moved. The large husky raised its ears and turned its head in the direction of the sound. Casey and Jon were in front of the house, on the other side and out of Ron's view. The dog took a step towards the sound, and then another, breaking into a slow methodic trot. It was a haughty run, as if the dog knew that it didn't need to needlessly waste energy on such an easy target. Another dog sprang and followed the big husky, then another. Janet spun, racing back down the hall.

"*CASEY AND JON!!*" she screamed, flying into the parlor, speeding towards the open front door. "*CASEY!!*

JON!! GET IN HERE!! GET IN HERE NOW!!"

Meanwhile, Ron had leapt off the back steps of the summer kitchen, bounding through the grass and around the house. The dogs paid no attention to him and easily out ran him in the distance to the front of the structure.

Janet flew out the front door. Jon carried his coffee can under his arm and Casey held her slug in her hand as the two, totally unaware of any danger whatsoever, climbed up the steps. Both children's mouths were open and they had a shocked look of disbelief, a *'what did we do now?* kind of expression. Janet caught movement out of her eye but didn't take the time to look. She whisked the children across the porch and into the house, slamming the front door closed behind her.

In the grass in front of the lighthouse the dogs stopped, sniffing the ground where the children had been playing. Janet could see them clearly now. All were dirty and unkept from living in the wild. Their ribs showed as they walked and the dogs looked sickly, as if they had been stricken by disease. The Doberman pawed at the ground and licked at the dirt for a moment, then stopped.

Another sound had caught their attention.

Ron had made it to the front of the lighthouse and he stopped, his eyes darting back and forth across the grass and the front of the building, praying that he didn't see Casey or Jon or Janet.

Thank God, he thought. *They made it. They made it in.*

The dogs stood frozen, watching Ron. Ron made no movement himself. He just stood there, watching the dogs watching him.

The husky moved.

It took one single slow step forward...a mocking, arrogant motion that reeked of arrogance and power. In that single step the husky displayed its dominance, gloating in its own boastful, radiant glory. The dog *knew*. The dog knew that the battle had been won before it had begun.

The German Shepard cocked its head and closed its mouth and, like the husky, took a step towards Ron. For the moment, it was a stand-off.

Without turning his head or even moving his eyes, Ron looked around to find an escape route. The front door of the lighthouse was out of the question. The dogs were only a few feet from the porch, and Ron would literally be running into the pack. Or if he turned and ran back to the summer kitchen, the dogs could surely overtake him easily. Sickly or not, they were far too fast and powerful for Ron to be able to get any distance on them.

The husky began to growl. It was a low, rumbling snarl that emanated from the depths of its chest. It curled its lips back, exposing upper and lower rows of dirty yellow incisors, honed sharp from years of use. Foamy saliva oozed from the sides of its mouth, dripping on to the ground. But there was something about the animal that made it appear even more menacing. The deep, dark eyes, and the way the animal just stood there, staring at him. The dog displayed too much confidence, too much arrogance, as if there was nothing on earth that could stop him. The dog was viciously alive, but at the same time, he was-

Dead?

Was that it? Was it dead? Were they all dead?

Ron continued to gaze into the demonic snarling faces that leered back at him. Their eyes were lifeless and empty, yet filled with fire, filled with wickedness and evil. He had never seen that look in an animal before, not ever. His eyes focused again on the husky while his mind frantically planned some way of escape. He knew for certain that he couldn't make it to the front door. And although the summer kitchen was behind him, he dared not turn his head to see how far. He was certain that the dogs would easily overtake him if he tried to run back. But maybe-

The tower.

Still keeping his eyes on the sneering pack of dogs Ron scanned his peripheral vision, estimating how many steps it would take to reach the conical tower. The door was unlocked and cracked open a bit as he had left it not ten minutes ago. The tower stood behind and to his left, some thirty feet away.

There was no more thinking. If he waited any longer and the dogs made the first move, they would have an extra step toward him. A step that Ron didn't have and couldn't afford to lose.

In a single motion he spun and bolted, focusing his eyes on the heavy wood door of the conical tower. As he did the dogs exploded, a seething hungry pack of ravenous animals howling and snarling, tearing through the grass.

CHAPTER SEVEN

Posavic was wrong. There weren't hundreds or even *thousands* of drawings and writings. There were *tens* of thousands of pages that had been authored by McClure. Pearson flipped through the single manilla folder in his hand. He pulled another drawing out and stared at it. It was a single tree, drawn in the center of the paper. Unlike the drawing of the lighthouse, this tree looked as if it were quickly scribbled without much thought. It was sloppy and hurried and looked more like a child's stick figure drawing.

The drawing on the next page was very similar, only drawn in different colors.

But the old doctor was right about one thing. Most of the writing that McClure had done made absolutely no sense. Virgil just ran inane words together that had no pattern of flow. There were no commas or periods, no paragraphs. It appeared that everything he'd written was one enormous run-on sentence that had no beginning and no end, but rather looped around to continue endlessly. Pearson scoured through page after page, trying to find some format to the madness, but found none. Emil had warned Pearson that most of McClure's writing had been as such, but he'd also said that there were times when he'd written very detailed accounts of stories or ideas.

Pearson opened another folder and flipped though the numerous drawings and pages of handwritten text. Still, he found no pattern or scheme. He tried to read what he thought might be a sentence, but the words just continued to jumble on by, not making any-

"Hold on there, Tom," he whispered aloud to himself. *"Whatta we got here?"* His eyes had caught a word but had darted to another page before comprehending what it was. Now he flipped back and looked for it.

Well I'll be a son of a gun, he thought. Tom stared at the word on the paper.

Naw. Prob'ly just a coincidence. There's a couple different meanings for that word.

He was about to flip the page over and look at the next one, but he stopped. The same word was again scribbled near the bottom of the same page.

Borders.

Tom's heart beat faster as he scanned the rest of the page, going over every word. His eyes glanced back and forth from one to the other. There was something different about the way the word was spelled or written.

No, that's not it, he thought. *It's spelled right. There's just something different about it that-*

Borders.

"That's it," he said aloud. Again, he scoured the page, comparing the word 'Borders' to other words. He looked on the next page.

Hidey-Ho. Whatta we got here? The word 'Borders' was again written in the same fashion that it had been written on the previous page.

The damned thing's got a capital 'B' he thought. He searched the page but he found no other words that began with capital letters. He continued searching the following pages and found the word 'Borders' written over a dozen times. It was the only word that began with a capital letter. He found dozens of words that should have been capitalized but weren't. 'Borders' was the only one.

Then, Virgil McClure just stopped. Pearson looked through twenty pages without finding the word again. All in all, McClure had written the word 'Borders' fifty-three times in thirteen pages. It was far too many times to be a simple coincidence. Especially since each of the fifty-three times McClure had written the word 'Borders' it began with a capital letter. Pearson searched and searched, but found no more capital letters anywhere in any other word on any other of the thirteen pages. It was as if a window opened up in McClure's brain, opening wide, then closing as quickly as it had emerged.

But if Pearson had been surprised by what he found on the thirteen pages, it was to be nothing compared to what he was about to find in the next folder.

Ron's feet pounded the ground, his eyes focused on the door of the conical tower. Normally he would have locked the door of the tower to keep Jon and Casey from curiously wandering up the stairs. But this time he had left it unlocked, and even open about an inch. It was his only chance.

Claws dug into the ground not twenty feet behind him. The dogs were at a full-blown run now and with every bound they were closing the gap between pack and prey. Ron could hear their howls of anticipation, their snarls of fury and anger.

He hit the brick conical tower with such force that he almost fell backwards. He recovered instantly, slipping one arm through the open door and throwing it open.

The huge husky leapt.

Ron bounded through the open door and grasped the doorknob on the inside, pulling it shut. The husky flew through the air and hit the wood chest-first, slamming the door closed. The animal fell to the ground but returned to its feet in an instant, tearing furiously at the door with its claws. The other dogs reached the door and they followed suit, snarling with indignation and rage. Ron could hear them on the other side of the door, swarming madly about the conical tower, seething in anger. His heart wailed like a base drum and his breathing was short and shallow from the frantic run across the yard.

He sprinted up the swirling steps two at a time. Beneath him, outside the safety of the tower, he could hear the dogs running angrily around, barking and howling, taunting their prey for one last chance, for one more opportunity. He shuddered at the thought. If there had been a mere split second lost while running to the tower...just a fraction of an instant...he wouldn't have made it. The pack of dogs would have been upon him, tearing and gnashing, attacking with razor sharp fangs. It would have been the end of the line for him.

Ron reached the top of the tower and looked down. The dogs had stopped and were staring upward, as if they had expected him to be there. They didn't even look real in the hazy, gray mist. Just dark shapes, frozen to the ground, motionless and still, like dirty stone statues at the base of the white tower.

Ron took his eyes off the pack and looked around the small room that housed the light. There were various objects scattered about the floor and on shelves, and at his feet he found just what he was looking for.

An old, heavy wrench that had been used to tighten and release the bolts that secured the light lay propped against the wall. It was almost eighteen inches long, and Ron picked it up and held it over the side of the tower.

"Let's see how much you little bastards like this," he muttered quietly. He drew the wrench back over his shoulder and let it fly. The wrench plummeted downward, twisting and turning in mid-air, speeding towards the pack below. The dogs remained frozen, looking up, watching Ron leaning over the railing atop the tower.

The heavy wrench took one bounce off the brick tower and spun madly, catching the Doberman square in the face. The dog yelped and fell sideways, distracting the other dogs from their prey atop the tower. The dog yapped in pain, rolling about on the ground, violently shaking its head, scratching its face with its paws. Even through the fog Ron could see the pool of blood beginning to stain the ground as the dog struggled, twisting in agony.

The remaining six dogs looked on, unmoving. The Doberman continued to writhe in pain, squealing from the painful blow to the face. The wrench had broken the dog's jaw and taken out one of its eyes, in addition to cracking its skull. The animal lay on the ground and began to convulse, shaking beyond control.

The husky looked up at Ron and the stern gaze between man and beast seemed to last an eternity. In a blue eye and a black eye, Ron saw hatred that burned and welled from a place unimaginable. The frenzy that blazed behind those penetrating eyes was nothing like Ron had ever seen. They were terrifying and beastly, but at the same time there was something so sickeningly familiar, so hauntingly human in those same eyes. They were the eyes of a world gone mad, a world of wretched evil and abhorrence. They glared back at Ron with wicked resentment and remorse. It was in that instant that Ron knew beyond any shadow of a doubt that the dogs were indeed dead, that the malevolence and bitterness in those eyes could in no way be a reflection of life of any kind. They were the untouchable eyes of the living dead, aflame with jealous rage and hysteria.

In the next moment the pack was upon the Doberman, ripping into its leathery skin and tearing at its flesh. It was uncontrollable mayhem as the dogs turned on one of their own, savagely attacking the mortally wounded dog. They battled one another for positions like a litter of pigs suckles their mother. The pathetic wailing and squealing continued until the big husky forced its mouth around the dying dogs' neck, and with one powerful snap the Doberman let out a piercing wail and then fell silent. Its body shuddered and grew limp, and the husky shook the Doberman one last time before releasing it. Another dog leapt forward, sinking its teeth into its tough rump. He began dragging the dead animal and now the rest of the pack joined in, pulling the dead dog away from the conical tower. Soon the ravenous dogs were lost in the fog, and the only thing Ron could hear were the excited shrieks and howls as the pack dragged the slain dog across the meadow and into the woods. The silence grew as the yelping slowly faded off. The sounds of the frenzied animals soon died away completely, and only the soft muffled whispering of a light breeze through the trees could be heard.

Below him he heard the front door of the lighthouse open. Janet's voice nervously called out, echoing up to him.

"Ron? Are you all right?"

He could see her dark figure through the fog as she leaned forward on the porch, not wanting to get too far from the door.

"I'm fine," Ron called out to her. "Go back in and close the door. The dogs are in the woods...but they might be back."

"Be careful, okay?" she responded, her voice shaking. It was more of a plea than a request. Ron acknowledged her simply by nodding his head a bit. Janet disappeared back into the lighthouse, closing the front door behind her. Ron, still at the top of the tower, listened intently and strained to hear anything from the pack. He heard nothing.

He hurriedly bounded down the stairs and cracked open the door, poking his head out and looking out over the meadow towards the trees where the dogs had gone. Still not seeing or hearing anything he snapped the door open and broke into a run, dashing towards the porch, every so often glancing behind him expecting to see the vicious pack on his heels. They never came, and he leapt over the porch. Janet had been watching and opened the door quickly as he reached it, slamming it closed behind him. Both he and Janet stood at the window looking out, expecting the dogs to appear at the edge of the forest, swaggering across the field towards the house. They never returned. Janet turned towards Ron, tears welling up in her eyes.

"What is going *on* here?" she whispered. Her voice cracked, and a tear ran down her cheek. Ron pulled her close and held her.

"Why were those dogs mean, Dad?" Jon asked. He and Casey sat on the floor of the parlor, still in the same places their mother had told them to stay. Ron glanced down at him and answered by slowly shaking his head.

Outside, the fog grew thicker and the sky grew darker as the storm crept closer to the island.

Pearson held the folder carefully in his hands as if it were china, as if he were afraid that one careless move would send the priceless piece tumbling out of his grasp and shattering on the cold cement floor. He squinted, straining to read the finely penciled letters on the worn paper.

It was an essay or a journal of sorts, and it actually made sense. Or, at least as much sense as you'd expect a lunatic to make. There were actual sentences, commas, periods, and paragraphs. Aside from a few misspelled words and a few 'i's that hadn't been dotted, Virgil McClure's grammar had taken a turn for the better. It was neat and smooth, so very different from the previous hundreds of pages that it looked as if it were written by someone else. Pearson carefully compared letters and words to make sure that McClure had indeed written the pages himself.

Christopher Knight

It began with Virgil writing all about what it was like growing upon the island, how he loved it there but hated everyone on it. He hated the children at school who had teased him, hated the schoolteacher, and even most (if not all) of the other adults there. His mother had died when Virgil was very young, and he had missed her terribly. Even his father was gone more than he was home, leaving young Virgil at a very early age to tend to his baby brother.

Pearson turned the page. Here the writing described his younger brother in detail, how they would play together for hours and hours. At six years old, Virgil had been more of a father than a brother. Harmon was his responsibility, even at that age. Virgil loved Harmon deeply and the following pages chronicled many accounts of playing in the meadow, fishing, and making crude toys from pieces of wood. Virgil never mentioned Harmon's exact age, but Pearson guessed that he couldn't have been more than two or three years old.

Funny, he thought. *He writes about his little brother as if they were the same age.* Yet he knew that Virgil was three or four years older. And there was little or no mention of the elder McClure. In addition to his duties as keeper of the lighthouse Virgil's father earned extra money working on a fishing boat, so Pearson assumed that he was probably gone most of the time.

When Harmon took ill and died it had destroyed Virgil. The boy had been buried next to his mother in a modest cemetery just west of the small village, but Virgil wrote that he had dug up the grave and carried his dead brother home. Upon returning to the lighthouse and discovering the dead boy, Virgil's father returned the boy to his grave during the night when he had less of a chance of being seen. Apparently no one in the village had discovered that Virgil had dug up the grave, and his father was going to try and keep it that way. Finally, after Virgil had dug up Harmon a half dozen times, the elder McClure re-buried him in the swamp in an attempt to hide Harmon's body from Virgil. Virgil didn't explain how he'd found the grave, but once again he had dug it up and brought Harmon back to the house. Through the course of the events someone in the village had found out about young Virgil's grave-robbing. No one dared investigate, but the word had gotten out nonetheless and Virgil became the target of the local school children. He became an instant outcast with no friends and virtually no family.

Pearson shook his head. Again, he'd heard stories of similar nature but considered them just too ridiculous to be *completely* true. Every time someone told a story like that it just seemed to change, sometimes just a tiny bit, other times a lot...until the story was so different from what really happened that you couldn't discern fact from fiction. He'd always known that *some* weird shit had gone on at the lighthouse on the island, but to read it in old pages like this brought the stories to life with a realism that turned his stomach. In a way, Pearson felt bad for Virgil, being so young and having to deal with so much at his age. But then again, most normal kids don't go around digging up their dead siblings.

He heard a faint scraping and shuffling and jumped, looking down the long corridor of the dimly lit basement.

A small mouse scurried across the floor not ten feet from where Tom stood. It bounced quickly between two filing cabinets and disappeared.

Pearson looked back at the papers in his hands and continued reading. If it hadn't already, McClure's lunacy was obviously beginning to show, in much more dramatic fashion. Here was the prisoner, Virgil McClure, locked in a mental institution, waiting impatiently for the return of his brother. His writings continuously focused on the fact that Virgil *knew* Harmon was coming back. Or *'is'* coming back, according to the way he'd written it. He rambled on for pages on his theories of 'wandering spirits' and 'reincarnation.' He believed that somehow the lighthouse would make Harmon live again, that there was some power that existed not only in the structure but in Harmon as well. Virgil had elevated his dead brother to a god-like status, claiming that no one knew the day or the hour that Harmon would return, except Virgil himself. And he vented his frustration at being locked up in Portsmouth, of being contained beyond his will. He felt it was his duty to make the island ready, to prepare for Harmon's inevitable return. Virgil expressed outrage that the lighthouse was being allowed to fall apart over the years. He believed that there was some mysterious power, some force within the lighthouse that would bring Harmon back, but it wouldn't be until the lighthouse had been re-conditioned to its original state. There needed to be some kind of a caretaker, some keeper that would oversee the reconstruction of-

Suddenly and without warning the lights went out.

Pearson snapped his head around in the dark, reaching for the flashlight on top of the filing cabinet. He clicked it on.

"Who's there?" he said aloud. His voice echoed down the corridor and immediately the lights blinked back on. He heard footsteps on the stairs from the far end of the corridor, and soon a uniformed guard appeared. Seeing Tom's uniform, the guard apologized.

"Sorry about that," the voice echoed back. "I guess I didn't know anyone was still down here. How long you gonna be, eh?"

"Not much longer," Tom replied. "Prob'ly just a few more minutes."

"Sure thing." The guard turned and walked back up the steps.

When Pearson looked back at the papers in his hand, he saw that the page he was reading had fallen to the floor. He bent down to pick it up, then stopped cold.

The following page was a drawing. Not only was it a drawing, but it was a portrait. It was a pencil sketch, in great detail. The drawing was a man's face, and it was drawn with such precision that it actually looked like a black and white photograph. The lines of the man's face were distinct and clear, and each individual hair on the man's head and eyebrows were defined with incredible detail. Then, below the drawing, a one-word inscription in capital letters:

HARMON M.

That's ridiculous, Pearson thought. *Harmon died when he was a boy. This is a man. An old man at that.* Still, the face looked vaguely familiar. Tom stared at the drawing, trying to put a name...*another* name...with the face.   The picture most certainly couldn't be Harmon McClure. And it wasn't Virgil, either. Pearson had seen a few pictures of him in old files, and the drawing he held was definitely not a self-portrait.

Maybe it's what Virgil thought he might look like, Tom thought. *That's it. That's just what Ol' Virgil imagined that Harmon would look like at that age.*

He turned the page.

The flashlight immediately fell from his hand, smashing in to a dozen pieces. The sound echoed down the corridor and quickly faded away, but the event went by unnoticed. Pearson held the paper in his hands and began to shake. It was another drawing, another immaculate sketch. No, it was more than a sketch. It *had* to be. It was unmistakable. The hair, the eyes. Even the stubble of growth on the man's cheeks. There was absolutely no mistake at all who the man was.

And Virgil had known. Somehow he had known years ago, locked up in an institution, locked away to write his nonsensical ravings and draw his obscure pictures. It was impossible, but he had known then. And the proof lay in large letters beneath the drawing.

BORDERS.

Pearson could do nothing but stare. The man's face stared back, and the caption seemed to scream off the page as Tom tried to keep his hands from shaking.

BORDERS.

The face of Ron Borders looked up at him from a page in time before Ron had probably even been born. It was the same face Tom had seen this morning, standing in the summer kitchen sipping a glass of whiskey.

It was *him.*

*But if...*Tom wondered, his thought suspended while he flipped the page back one.

If that's Ron Borders...then who the hell is this?

By one o'clock the fog showed no signs of lifting, and Ron felt that it was almost certainly the precursor to the storm that Pearson had talked about. The air was thick and cold and low clouds wisped about the house and the conical tower, sheathing the island of St. Helena like a damp gray blanket. Ron and Janet stood in the parlor while Jon nibbled on the last of a sandwich on the floor. Casey had grown tired and fallen asleep, and she lay huddled among a half dozen burlap and canvas bags that contained their clothing and other items that they would be taking with them today. Ron had tucked another pile of items away in the summer kitchen to be picked up when he returned in a week or two. Ron stared out the window as he spoke.

"We have to warn him somehow," he said blankly.

"The radio won't work?" Janet asked.

"No. Just static. Maybe when this fog clears."

"But he'll be here in a few hours. What if the dogs find

him?" Janet shuddered at the thought of them walking around the old village, the children playing in the yard...all while a hungry pack of wild dogs roamed freely over the island.

"He's got a gun. I think he'll be okay even if we don't get ahold of him."

Jon finished his sandwich and now he too was nodding off to sleep next to Casey. Ron and Janet watched out the windows.

And waited.

The telephone clicked in Tom's ear, and then a series of loud tones barked from receiver.

We're sorry...all circuits are busy at this time. Please-
Pearson slammed the receiver down on the hook, picked up the phone, and dialed the number to the Mackinaw County Sheriff's Department again. Once more the same tones blared from the small speaker.

"How do all the circuits up here get *busy?!?!*" Tom wondered aloud. The receptionist seated at the front desk overheard and looked up.

"School's just getting out. Every kid with a modem is at home getting on the Internet. We've been having problems for the past few months, ever since more and more people started getting on line. There's just not enough telephone lines to support all the calls. Not yet, anyway." The woman was polite but went back to her business immediately, which at the moment was filing her nails with a long emery board that looked like it would be more suited to sharpen a steak knife.

Pearson walked back down the hall towards Posvic's office. Emil was still gone and Tom couldn't wait for him to return. He scribbled a note and left it on his desk, saying that it would be important that he call him as soon as he got in. He wasn't going to leave a note telling the doctor that he'd taken some of Virgil's drawing and writings, but he would have to let him know. He peeped his head out of the office to make sure no one was watching, and then he quickly stuffed a dozen of McClure's writings and drawings under his shirt. Pearson was certain that the hospital administration would not allow him to take the articles, and in this case it would be better to ask for forgiveness than to try and cut through the red tape and ask for permission. It was already three o'clock; he didn't have the time for formalities.

He waved to the security guard who had escorted him in. The guard opened the door and led Pearson across the parking lot to the patrol car. After a brief inspection Pearson was allowed to exit the parking lot through the fence, winding through the lush green grass. The small stack of papers stashed beneath his shirt was uncomfortable and he pulled them out and plopped them on the passenger seat as he drove.

There were three or four 'patients' wandering the

grounds, and one by one they each stopped what they were doing to watch the car glide across the lawn on the black driveway. A man wearing a blue jumpsuit was trimming hedges near the building. He stopped and waved at Tom in slow motion, rocking his arm gently back and forth like a giant blue Koala bear. Tom managed a brief smile and waved back.

If he hadn't turned his head back to the driveway right at that moment, it would have been all over. Pearson slammed the brake pedal to the floor, locking up the tires and screeching to a sudden halt. He hadn't seen the man leap out from behind the tree and run onto the road and into the path of the oncoming car. The vehicle squealed to a stop but the man remained in the middle of the road, glaring at Tom through the windshield. He was old and bedraggled and his hair was messy and strewn about his head like an old mop. He was thin and scrawny and the features of his face were like stone, as if his skull was about to poke through his pale skin. Like the other people in the yard the man wore a dull blue jumpsuit, but it appeared to be much too big for him. It sagged over his shoulders like a loose burlap sack and the sleeves hung past his knuckles. He remained standing in front of the patrol car, apparently unaware at how close he had come to death. If the car would have traveled just another six inches it would have struck the man.

Pearson waited. There were rules to be followed, and this was one of them. Second page, third paragraph in the Portsmouth Visitors and Guest Policy: *Remain in your vehicle at ALL times. If you need assistance, wait for staff security to arrive. Keep all doors locked and windows closed. NEVER leave your vehicle for ANY reason.*

The old man continued to glare at him through the windshield. He opened his mouth slowly, revealing an upper row of decaying, rotting teeth. Apparently oral hygiene was not a top priority at Portsmouth. Tom considered backing up and going around the man but again remembered the rules. Portsmouth was strict about their regulations, and if a Sheriff's Deputy couldn't comply, who else would?

Suddenly the man leaned forward and placed one hand on the hood. He was *speaking*. His voice was barely a whisper and Tom couldn't make out what he was saying. The man appeared to struggle with the words as if he were speaking for the first time, learning to sound out vowels and consonants while at the same time trying to grasp their meaning. Tom watching intently, watching the man's lips as he continued.

Then, he *could* hear a voice. The man began speaking louder and now he raised a thin, scrawny arm and pointed a bony finger at Tom.

It was then that Pearson recognized him. It had been a long time. A long, long time...but there was no mistake. The frightened, wild eyes. The high, piercing cheekbones. And the thick, pointed nose that looked oddly misplaced on such a thin, frail face. It was the face of the one and only Fred Overmeyer.

Pearson remembered the folder that he had skimmed through the previous night, recalling the events of 1968 that led to Overmeyer being incarcerated at Portsmouth in the first place. Fred of course had denied everything, resting on his defense that the lighthouse killed his brother and the two hired workers. The story made front page news around the country until Fred Overmeyer was found incompetent to stand trial. On trial for what charges no one knew. No bodies were found, there was no murder weapon, no motive. Just the missing people and the words of a lunatic. Fred Overmeyer was shipped up to Portsmouth and the world had long forgotten him and his crazy stories.

"He tried to tell us," Overmeyer wheezed, leaning farther over the hood, glaring at Tom. His voice was strained and raspy, the sound of an old woman who had spent her life drinking vodka and smoking cigarettes. He hissed like a snake, and his eyes quivered as he spoke.

"But we wouldn't listen," he continued. *"Nobody listened."* With that, Fred Overmeyer leaned away from the vehicle and stumbled over to the drivers' side window. His face was nearly pressed to the glass as he bent down and his crazy, wild eyes bulged out of their sockets, leering at the deputy. Tom glanced in the rearview mirror. On the other side of the locked parking fence he could see commotion and men running about.

"He came back, didn't he?" Overmeyer hissed. *"DIDN'T HE!?!?"*

Tom just stared, watching Overmeyer's face glaring back at him just inches from the window. His hand clasped the nine millimeter pistol at his waist.

"I knew he would," Overmeyer continued. *"It was just a matter of time. It was always...just...a matter of time."*

In the rearview mirror Pearson could see the gate

opening and a truck pull though. Two men rode in the back leaning over the top of the cab and another two rode inside.

"I knew he'd come back," Overmeyer repeated. *"I always knew he'd come back. And you did too, dincha? That's why you're here, isn't it? You're tryin' to figure it all out, aren'tcha? Well now that he's here, what are ya gonna do? I'll tell ya whatcher gonna do. Nothin'. Yer not gonna do nothin', because you can't. You don't know how. You don't know-"*

He stopped suddenly, staring at the car seat on the other side of Pearson. Tom glanced at the rearview mirror to see the truck getting closer, then looked down at the seat where Overmeyer was staring. It was Virgil's sketch of Harmon.

The old man backed away from the car, his mouth gaping, his eyes bulging even wider. His face began to shake and saliva began to drool from the side of his mouth. Overmeyer fell to his knees, glaring at Tom. He was trying to speak, trying to say something, but no words came out. Spittle ran down his chin and dripped to the grass as he knelt, shaking with fright. The seizure gripped Overmeyer like a vise and his entire body shook out of control.

In the next instant two men appeared out of nowhere, tackling Overmeyer and holding him to the ground face first. He put up no struggle or fight as the men handcuffed him and lifted him back to his knees. Another man hustled up and shackled his legs. Overmeyer had yet to take his eyes off Pearson, and only when he was led away to the truck was he forced to turn his gaze elsewhere.

A uniformed security officer approached the car and knocked on the window. Pearson rolled it down.

"Everything all right, sir?" the man asked.

"Sure, fine," Tom responded. "No problem."

"Sorry about your delay." With that the man turned and walked back to the truck. Tom let his foot off the brake and the patrol cruiser slowly continued along the winding blacktop, stopping only to allow the front gate to swing open for him.

The patrol car flew along US-2 and Pearson every so often flashed his lights to alert drivers ahead of him to pull off the road. He sped by all of them, and most were just thankful that the patrol car passed by and just kept on going. Pearson was oblivious to the traffic as thoughts kept spinning through his head. There were too many questions, too many coincidences...none of which made the least bit of sense. The sickening, twisted face of Fred Overmeyer haunted him as trees flew past.

How had Overmeyer known? Pearson thought. *How did he know that I was at Portsmouth? How did he know what was going on?*

Without warning a white-tailed deer suddenly leapt from the shoulder of the highway and Tom swerved, slamming on his brakes for the second time that day. The animal bolted across the pavement and disappeared into the thick brush. Pearson glanced to both sides of the highway, wary of any more deer, reminding himself to take it easy, take it slow, be careful. In another five minutes he was back at a healthy ninety-five miles per hour, the image of the deer completely forgotten. His mind was spinning, reeling with questions and confused thoughts.

How had Virgil McClure known what Ron Borders looked like? he thought over and over again. *Or rather...what he was* going *to look like?* Pearson had carefully inspected the paper, certain that it was quite old. There was no way anyone had drawn a recent picture and placed it in the file. Hell, the cabinet looked like it hadn't been opened in forty years. No, the drawings were old, the writings were old...*but what were they supposed to mean? How would someone know the name and facial features of a man that probably hadn't been born yet?* It was all too bizarre to even guess. *And why did Fred Overmeyer completely wig out over the drawing of Harmon...or whoever the hell he was? Was it supposed to be Ron? Was Ron Borders supposed to be the 'reincarnated' Harmon McClure?* It was far too bizarre to even imagine. Pearson was a realist, and although he admitted that there might be more than a few things going on that he couldn't explain, reincarnation or the return of the dead weren't on the list. *That shit just don't happen,* he reminded himself. And Virgil had written the name 'Borders' fifty-three times within just a few-

Fifty-three times? Tom thought, adding numbers in his head. Virgil McClure died in 1945-

Exactly fifty-three years ago.

Christopher Knight

Ninety-five miles per hour became ninety-six, ninety-seven...one hundred. Pearson only slowed through some of the small towns that were sparsely dotted along the highway. The fog began to grow noticeably thicker as he approached St. Ignace, and off in the distance over his right shoulder the island of St. Helena was clouded and invisible, hidden within the ominous, dense mist.

He screeched to a stop in the parking lot of the Sheriff's Department and went straight to his office, trying to reach Ron on the radio but receiving no response. It was now nearing five o'clock, and he didn't have time to waste if he wanted to make it to the island before the storm moved in. In the parking lot he swapped his car for one of the new black Suburbans the Department had purchased and headed across town to the marina.

The repairs had taken most of the day and the crew at the marina had just finished their work. Tom backed the trailer down the ramp and loaded the boat. Normally he would have left for St. Helena Island right from the marina, but at this point it would be faster to trailer the boat to a small ramp near his house and launch it from there where the waves were still under two feet.

He backed the trailer down the crude boat launch that was part of a small public access site near his cabin. He launched the boat, tied it to the end of the dock, jogged back to the Suburban, parked both it and the trailer off to the side of the road, and jogged back to the boat. Visibility was still poor and Pearson could barely make out the outline of the island as he started up the boat and headed for St. Helena. He'd forgot to tell Ron that he'd have to pick him up on the north shore, where he had beached his boat last night. It would be too dangerous to try to come ashore from the southern part of the island where the lighthouse was. When the storm hit the rollers crashing in over there would be at least six feet high and the eighteen-foot patrol boat would be no match for the hurricane-like conditions, especially with two more adults, two kids, and whatever gear they were bringing with them. Pearson would beach the patrol boat in the safety of the northeast harbor near the village and hike the trail through the swamp over to the lighthouse.

Again he tried to reach Ron on the radio, but still got no answer. He told himself that everything was going to be just fine, that somehow this was all just a series of bizarre and coincidental circumstances. At least that's what he *told* himself. Unfortunately he knew better.

He pulled the throttle just a bit more, hoping for just a slight increase of speed that would get him to the island quicker. He glanced down at his watch.

5:45. Damn. Forty-five minutes late.

If he pushed it, he could make it to the harbor in twenty more minutes, then twenty more minutes through the swamp to the lighthouse, twenty minutes back to the boat...and even then they wouldn't have much time. The full brunt of the storm system loomed menacingly off to the west and already the waves that were smashing the hull were increasing in size, bullying the patrol boat and tossing it back and forth in the chaotic waters. It was going to be another repeat of the storm last night only probably worse, and he certainly didn't want to be on the water for *that.*

Thankfully, Pearson thought, they would be traveling *with* the waves on the return trip. It would be a little easier going, but still tricky nonetheless. He glanced back up at the island.

The St. Helena lighthouse was invisible beneath a blanket of thick fog, but the conical tower pierced through the mist, standing above the tiny island. Behind it the wall of dark, baleful clouds of the coming storm threatened. Pearson could see flashes of light in the clouds as lightning raged within the freshwater monsoon. It was as if the entire storm system had been draped in brilliant white Christmas tree lights, each tiny bulb periodically flashing brightly, reflecting off tinsel and other decorative ornaments in the tree. Only this was a cloud bank, an *enormous* one, and the tiny bulbs of light were jagged spears of electricity, spiraling and churning within the boiling clouds.

A wave slammed into the boat and sent Pearson plummeting to the deck face first. He bounded up in an instant, uninjured except for a bruised elbow that he'd used to break his fall. He rubbed at the soreness with one hand and grabbed the wheel with the other. He would have to hurry.

He glanced up at the small harbor now becoming more visible through the thick gray curtain of fog, then looked up at the tower in the distance. The light was lit again, and a tiny dark figure stood just outside the lantern room on the observation deck, standing watch over the gathering storm.

"This is Ron Borders calling Deputy Tom Pearson. Ron Borders calling Deputy Tom Pearson...." The radio cracked and sputtered, but there was no answer.

"Any luck?" Janet asked, turning to face Ron from where she sat in the parlor.

"No. Not a thing from anybody. I think the weather's really messed up the signal."

It was six o'clock, and Ron had yet to hear from the deputy. He'd stood in the parlor staring out the window for a long time, expecting at any moment to see Tom Pearson emerge from the tree line. Casey and Jon had awoken and were each saying their good-byes to their respective pets, as their father had told them that neither reptiles nor amphibians were going to be allowed to become members of the Borders' family. Casey was heartbroken, wondering how poor Squiggy would survive or fend for itself without her. Jon was equally distraught, as both children had planned on keeping their new-found friends forever. And both were saddened and confused when their mother told them earlier in the day that they would be leaving for good. Both wanted to know why.

"How come we can't stay?" Jon whined again, his snake curled up in a tiny ball in his palm. "Is it because of the mean dogs?" Ron ignored the repeated questions after he'd heard them a dozen times. He continued fiddling with the exterior antennae on the back of the radio, but still had no luck in getting it to work properly.

"Mom...why can't we stay?" Jon repeated, this time directing the question towards his mother.

"Because we *can't*," Janet answered, her irritation growing. She too had become tired with the children's repeated pleas and continued questions.

Casey's nose was pressed against the small baby food jar, watching her slug slowly climb down the side of the glass as she spoke.

"It's because he doesn't like Daddy isn't it?"

Both Janet and Ron froze. Ron had been rolling the radio over in his hands and Janet was packing a small box. They both stopped, staring at Casey. Jon absently fingered his snake as if he hadn't heard.

"Who doesn't like Daddy, sweetheart?" Janet asked, a milder sweeter tone in her voice. Casey heard her mother but she continued to stare at Squiggy, watching the creature slowly crawl down the side of the jar.

"Virgil McClure," she said matter-of-factly. *"Virgil wants to kill Daddy."*

On the second floor, a window shattered. The noise scared Jon and Casey, and the two children ran to their mother. Ron set the radio back on the table and flew up the stairs two at a time. He stopped at the top step and looked around.

Three of the doors were open and Ron went slowly from room to room, looking at each window. All were intact, unbroken and perfect as they had always been.

Except....

The crash had come from behind the locked door. Even

as he inspected each of the rooms, he was certain. He knew where the noise had come from.

Ron reached up above the molding and grabbed the skeleton key and forced it into the keyhole, opening the door in a frenzy. The door suddenly exploded open, smashing against the wall. It shook with repercussion and recoiled, quivered for a moment, then stopped. Ron's jaw fell, and he stared.

The room was entirely furnished. The odor that had been so prevalent only two days ago was gone, replaced by a sweet, summer-like smell. A child's bed lay against one wall, and a new rocking chair, also for a child, sat in the corner. The wood floor shined as if it had been sanded and coated with polyurethane, and the walls were painted a rich, bright yellow. The bed was neatly made and even the sheets and blankets were new. Wood toys were placed neatly in a toy box next to the rocker, and a dresser, polished like the day it was made, stood with majestic pride against the wall opposite the bed. It was if the room was *...ready*. Ready for someone. Everything was clean and perfectly in order, arranged with sanitary flawlessness. The only thing that wasn't perfect was-

The window.

A baby blue cotton curtain fluttered easily in the breeze. Below it on the floor, pieces of glass lay scattered about. Ron turned his head and gazed at the dresser. A photograph of a man standing atop the conical tower of the lighthouse was the only ornament decorating the bureau. It was the same photograph that Janet had showed him, only this one seemed to be new and much more detailed. Ron drew closer to the photo, staring intently at the man standing at the top of the conical tower.

Was it?

No, he told himself.

Could it be?

He took a quick glance around the room and took a step towards the bureau. The blue curtain billowed up from the wind, and somewhere outside, high above, a seagull screamed as it flew overhead.

He took another step towards the bureau, his eyes keenly focused on the framed picture. When Janet had found the photograph it had been worn and yellowed with age. The forms had been blurry and out of focus. Now, as Ron drew nearer, he could see the picture was sharp and crisp. He could see the outlines of the individual bricks of the conical tower. Inside the glass room atop, the light and its hardware was clearly visible. But it was the features of the man that stood out most.

The man in the picture standing atop the light gazing out over the lake was the man Ron had seen in the window. It was the same man that had stood in the tower last night as the storm raged. It was the man that held the lantern at the edge of the meadow as Ron stood atop the light, looking across the field.

Well, hoodja expect...Abraham Lincoln?

The voice seemed to echo through the room and Ron whirled, looking for the intruder, but there was no one there. He was alone in the room. Again the voice spoke to him.

Over here, Ronnie....

In disbelief Ron again turned to look at the picture. He could see the tightness in the man's cheeks, the firm jaw bone that jutted out from beneath the skin.

I toldja he was comin' back, didn't I?

The man in the picture turned.

"What in God's name...." Ron whispered aloud. His voice was cut short by the howling laughter in his head.

You know...that's real funny, Ron. I must have heard that expression a thousand times over the years, and it's STILL funny.

Ron's eyes were huge and his mouth was open, gazing in terror at the small figure in the picture. The man had a terrible smile, a fake smile like some demented circus clown. As Ron watched, the face of the man began to change, like it had in this same bedroom when he had first encountered this same man. Features distorted and twisted, and the man became a boy again, a young child no more than twelve, smiling sweetly, looking back at Ron.

See Ronnie? Oh, I'm sorry...I know you don't like 'Ronnie.' But your mother called you that, didn't she? She called you that right up until the day she died, didn't she? I myself know what death is like, Ronnie. Even I have tasted the stinging sensation of loss....

Ron began to shake as once again the features of the figure changed, in rapid succession this time. It became Ron's father, his mother, then the man again, back to the boy, then back to the man again.

"Who...who are you?" Ron managed to stammer. The man laughed, and the booming voice reverberated in the halls of Ron's head.

Oh come now, Mr. Borders. Surely you must have guessed by now.

Ron shook his head slowly, more in disbelief than as a physical answer.

Of course you know. Just who, Ron, has been repairing the lighthouse? Surely you don't believe it's been ALL you? Don't you think that maybe...just maybe...you had a little help? Do you really think you've done it alone? You see, I needed you, Mr. Borders. I needed your hands and your toil. You and I really do have a lot in common, you know. And while it is true you and I both have suffered terrible loss, I am about to experience the pure joy that you, Ron, will never know. You see, while you're loss is gone forever, mine....

The man began to smile and spoke very slowly.

-is about....

The small blue curtain lifted high as a strong breeze pushed it back from the broken window. Ron could hear the trees beyond the meadow shaking and trembling from the strong gust, and the bedroom door suddenly exploded behind him, slamming closed.

-to come back.

The man in the picture began to laugh. It was a haunting, screeching wail that pierced through the room, causing Ron to throw his hands over his ears. The laughter continued and suddenly Ron reached forward, sweeping the framed picture off the dresser and hurling it violently against the wall. The glass shattered into a thousand pieces and tiny bits and slivers erupted like shrapnel throughout the room. The laughter stopped, and the curtain sank quietly back in to place. It fluttered for only an instant, then froze. Outside the wind diminished and the trees were silent. The air was thick and damp, and a smell began to drift through the room, the very same stench that Ron had smelled two days previous. He felt something tap his head, and he reached up with his hand to rub his hair.

There was blood on his finger.

Ron looked up in time to see the next drop fall from the ceiling and plunk onto his forehead. He wiped it away quickly and stepped back as another drop fell and landed on the smooth wood floor.

Drip.

Another drop fell from the ceiling.

Drip.

A light scraping sound caught his attention. He looked at the broken shards of glass on the floor.

One of them moved. Then another. The glass was organizing itself into a neat pile on the floor as if it were being swept by some unseen broom. Ron watched, his eyes wide, too horrified to run.

A piece of glass broke away from the floor and snapped into the air. It crunched and squeaked as it returned to its exact place in the window pane. Then another piece of glass did the same, then another, and another. Pieces of the picture frame were doing the same. Within seconds, both the picture and the window were completely repaired. The picture snapped upright and flew back to its position on the bureau.

It was *perfect.* The frame had no imperfections at all, and it sat in the exact position it had been in when Ron had first entered the room.

He looked at the window.   There were no seams, no flaws, no blemishes. Like the picture frame it was now absolutely perfect.   The entire room was immaculate, barring the steadily increasing drips of blood that were falling from the ceiling above.

Ron broke out of his trance-like state and reached for the doorknob. It was locked and he pounded it with his fist.

"Janet!!" he screamed. *"Janet!! Help me open the door!!"* He gave the door a powerful kick and the hinge gave way, splintering into pieces. The door fell to the floor and Ron bounded over it, sailing down the stairs four at a time. Janet was on her way up, a confused, shocked look on her face.

"What is it?!? What's wrong?!?" She asked nervously, sensing the anxiety and tension in Ron's face.

"We're leaving. *Now.*" He placed both hands on her shoulders and turned her around, continuing down the stairs. "Casey! Jon! *Let's go!!!*" The children began to protest, but Ron interrupted.

"But Dad! I can't-" Ron didn't give Jon a chance to finish the sentence.

"I SAID NOW!!" He grabbed his son by the shoulder and pushed him out the door on to the porch. Janet picked up Casey and rushed her outside.

"Ron!! What is it!?!?" But Ron didn't answer. The house had started to tremble, a low rumble from within that was now beginning to shake the walls. He grabbed two duffle bags that were on the floor and leapt out the door, bounding off the porch and into the yard.

The rumbling slowly ceased until the shaking finally stopped completely. The lighthouse was quiet once again. Then, as if someone had thrown some unseen switch, the light atop the conical tower suddenly burst to life, shining like a brilliant yellow flare in the encroaching darkness.

Pearson reached the harbor and beached the boat, leaping to the shore and jogging up the shoreline. He walked quickly through the remains of the old town and found the trail that led through the swamp and across the island.

The wind blew furiously, bending the trees and tearing new leaves from their branches and hurling them wildly across the sky. It had been sprinkling lightly for the past hour or so, and Pearson knew that it would only be a matter of time before the sky opened up, cutting loose torrents of rain. Making it back to the mainland after that would be nearly impossible in the patrol boat. He would have to hurry.

He quickened his pace along the trail, half running as he swept the branches away from his face. Coming up on his left, on the other side of a thick hedge of trees, the towering cedar stood...or *the* towering cedar stood...bent sluggishly in the blustering gale, gouging at the sky like a soldier's bayonet. Tom remembered what Ron had said about the old grave last night, about the pickets and the stone, the cross and the blood. Pearson had seen the site on a few occasions and as he walked he peered through the dense branches to catch a glimpse of the pickets, not really knowing what to expect. In a strange, macabre sort of way, he wanted to see the new pickets, the grave stone and the cross. He wanted to see the blood seeping through the grass and soaking into the white, polished picket fence.

The young cedars were shuddering too much in the wind for him to get a look at the base of the old cedar, and he quickly zig-zagged off the path and stood before the line of trees. Only a crowded line of cedar saplings stood between him and the old grave site of Harmon McClure. Cautiously, he outstretched his hands and pulled away the branches.

The grave looked as it always had...aging, weather-beaten pickets standing in a rectangular box-like shape around the tree, some bent to one side or the other by seasons of snow and wind and rain. It really was amazing that the pickets had fared this long. They were gray and dirty, just as he'd remembered them to be. The unkept grass had grown up till it almost reached the tips of the pickets. He chuckled to himself as he stepped through the branches and stood next to the grave.

"No disrespect, Harmon," he muttered. *"But sorry 'bout yer luck."* He turned around and started back to the trail, shaking his head. *"You're in the ground and you ain't comin' back."*

He looked up and stopped, completely frozen.

They stood in a row, as if at attention, not twenty yards away. Eyes filled with hate and malice, tongues dripping with greed and fury. The dogs made not a move, not a sound. They just watched the uniformed man, waiting.

Ho-lee shit, Tom, he thought. *You gotcherself some troubles now.* The dogs continued to assess their prey, watching, waiting, waiting for the right moment. Slowly... very slowly...Tom started to reach for his gun. Still, the dogs made no movement.

If he would have lived to tell about it, he would have said that the sound behind him was like a sword being pulled carefully from a leather sheath. Soft, quiet. A whispering swish...just enough to make him turn slowly around to see what it was.

The tattered gray picket floated motionless in the air for a moment, fresh black soil dirtying the portion that had been buried in the ground. It hung in the air, spinning slowly like a graceful ballerina dancer, prancing round and round, round and round. It dangled like a child's mobile, turning and twisting as if it were attached to a tiny thread. Pearson had only a split second of comprehension before the picket shot towards him in a blinding fury, plunging into his right eye. He screamed in horrible agony and fell to his knees, grasping the picket with both hands, trying to pull the wooden harpoon from his face. Another picket emerged from the ground and sailed toward him, piercing his leg. He recoiled and stood up, still grasping the picket in his eye, screaming from the searing pain. Another picket shot from the ground, and another, both of them piercing the tender skin of his legs and plunging deep into his flesh.

Pearson fell to his knees again, his strength draining. Blood gushed from his eye socket, the gray picket still lodged forcefully in his skull. Another picket snapped up from the ground, spun in the air a moment as if taking aim, then rocketed towards him, impaling Pearson's genitals and burying itself in his groin. It twisted and turned as it forced its way deeper and deeper within, finally piercing the outer skin of his buttocks. Pearson fell to the ground curled in a fetal position, dizzy from the caustic, burning pain. He struggled to move but couldn't find the strength. His brown uniform was soaked with blood, and his face was painted completely red. One final picket slowly emerged from the ground and floated over him, waiting, waiting for him to move, daring him to even flinch a muscle. Pearson was aware of it, but the fuzziness in his mind was beginning to take over as he started to lose consciousness. He could see the line of dogs, still standing as they had always been, unmoving and motionless. One eye slowly glanced up at the dirty gray javelin suspended above him. It danced in the air, taunting, daring, waiting for the deputy to make a move. Then, in that final moment of life, Virgil's drawing of Harmon McClure popped into his mind. The face flashed before him and he now *knew* why it had looked so familiar. The hair, the cheekbones, the old lines on his brow. He could see the man's face clearly in his mind, both as a drawing and as a real person. And he realized, perhaps far too late, that Virgil had been right. Virgil had known. Fred Overmeyer had known. And Jerry Hartmann and Raymond Cooper.

Harmon McClure was coming back to St. Helena.

The face in his mind took a life of its own, laughing at Pearson as he lay dying on the ground, a twirling dagger above him ready to strike. Harmon's demonic laughter filled his head and roared in his ears.

No disrespect, Tom, the voice mocked. *But sorry 'bout yer luck....*

Suddenly the spinning picket above him launched itself downward, spearing violently into Pearson's temple, driving into his skull, though squishy brain tissue and out the other side of his head, burying itself once again into the ground.

The entire supernatural execution had taken less than a minute. Tom Pearson lay on the forest floor, his lifeless body twisted in agony, his years reduced to nothing more than a bloody pincushion at the foot of the huge cedar tree. Instantly the frenzied pack was upon him, swarming and snapping at soft flesh, howling and snarling with gluttonous passion. They dragged Tom Pearson's limp body into the shadows, into the dark of the thick cedar swamp.

CHAPTER EIGHT

Ron and Janet looked back up at the lighthouse. The light shined brightly, brilliantly against the darkening clouds. Tiny sprinkles of rain fell and the wind blew strongly, thrashing the trees and sending large waves to pummel the white sandy shoreline. It began to rain harder and they ran, Janet carrying Casey, to the shelter of the large oak tree. Ron dashed to the shore, looking out over the raging Straits of Mackinac.

The sweetwater sea was in turmoil. Angry whitecaps

snarled over the bay, lashing upwards, biting and entangling one another. The waves battered back and forth, leaping towards the clouds in a raging fury. The fog had dissipated, replaced by a dark, charcoal sky. The thick gray canopy boiled with destruction, harnessing mighty winds and bursting with devastating charges of electricity that thundered angrily within the bulging, churning clouds. The storm was going to be altogether everything that last night's storm had been and more. Ron dashed back to the tree where Janet and the children stood.

"We can't stay here," Ron spoke loudly over the wind.

"Where is the Sheriff's boat?!?!" Janet stammered. Deputy Pearson should have been here over an hour ago."

"I don't kn-" Ron suddenly realized that there was no way that the patrol boat would be able to reach them on this side of the island. Pearson wouldn't even attempt it. He would arrive in the harbor at the village like he had last night, where it would be less windy and the waves wouldn't be slamming into the shore as hard as they were on this side of the island.

"Lets go. I'm sure he's over there. It's the only place he could be." He looked around. *"Where's Jon?"*

Janet had been holding Casey and watching her husband through the trees and hadn't seen Jon wander off.

"Jonny forgot his snake," Casey chimed in, pointing across the meadow towards the lighthouse.

In complete horror, Ron and Janet spun and looked across the darkening meadow. Jon had just reached the porch.

"JON!! NO!!!" Ron screamed.

But it was too late. Jon was bounding up the steps, over the porch, and....

Inside.

Instantly the door slammed shut behind him. Ron took off running towards the house.

"Stay here!" he yelled back at Janet as he burst away from the tree. He was running, tearing over the meadow through the wet grass, and he leapt on to the porch and slammed into the front door of the lighthouse. The door held fast and Ron bounced back, grabbing the doorknob and turning it. It was locked. He pounded on the door with his fists.

"Jon!! Jon!! Open the door!" It began to rain harder and the wind grew stronger just within the past few moments. Ron could hear Jon on the other side of the door.

"I...I can't get it open," Jon said from inside the house. The doorknob jiggled a bit, but it held fast. Ron tried harder, but the doorknob wouldn't budge. He began kicking at the door.

"Get back!" he yelled. *"Get away from the door!"* He kicked violently at the door as well as the doorknob, but it was far too strong. It was as if the door was-

Ron looked closer. It *was*. It *was* brand new. This wasn't the same door they had left just a few minutes ago. *That* door had been old and gray, but this door was a rich red-brown. And every bit as solid as the tree that it came from. The door was literally a brand new door.

He ran around to the side of the house, glancing back to check on Janet and Casey. His wife still held their daughter in her arms, holding her face to her shoulder to prevent her from seeing the malevolent, disturbing scene. Ron picked up a rock the size of a softball and sent it hurdling towards the window, but the heavy stone did nothing more than bounce off the glass and on to the ground. He picked up the rock and tried again, with the same results.

The ground began to shake. Ron could feel it tremble beneath him, jerking and swaying in short bursts. He could hear Jon inside, running frantically about the parlor.

"Dad...what's happening...Dad?"

"Get over by the front door and stay there!" Ron yelled. He picked up an old piece of pipe and smashed it through the window. The glass exploded and fragments tinkled to the floor inside the lighthouse, but in a split second the tiny pieces were airborne again, crunching and snapping back into place. The window...*the house*...was repairing itself. Ron tried to break the window again as the glass flew back into place, but his efforts were in vain. In seconds the window was brand new.

The ground around the house began to shake and rock, and Ron felt like he were in an earthquake. He struggled to keep his balance as the house creaked and moaned above him. It was as if...if the house was *breathing*. Ron could sense the deep inhaling and exhaling, the in and out, in and out *whooshing* as if the house was gasping for air like the heaving chest of someone who had stayed under the water too long and was just reaching the surface.

"Dad...something...something's happening...." The tone in his son's voice was shaky and trembling as if he knew something awful were about to take place.

"Dad...there's something in here...."

Ron stepped closer to the house and glared through a window. Jon was backed against the door, a horrified expression on his face. He clutched the Maxwell House can with both arms, pulling the metal container against his chest. His eyes were darting frantically from wall to wall. Ron looked the room over.

And there he was.

At the far end of the hall, the man stood watching, smiling, as if supervising the entire macabre scene.

Sorry Ron, the voice said, the man's lips frozen in the same wicked, malevolent grin. *It's just that I've missed him for so long. And he's coming back. They said he never would, but they were wrong. He'll be back soon now. Very soon. It will be so good to see him again.*

"YOU AREN'T TAKING HIM!!" Ron screamed, pounding at the widows with his fists. *"DO YOU HEAR ME!?!? YOU AREN'T TAKING HIM!!!"*

Sorry Ronnie. That's just the way it's got to be. It's just a swap, that's what it is. A friendly swap. You lose...and I win. Another wicked roar of laughter bawled through the house, resounding off the walls and ceiling. The sound became one with the driving wind and the rapidly approaching thunder and Virgil McClure raised his eyebrows, winked at Ron, and vanished.

See ya, buddy boy.

Inside the parlor a red stain had begun seeping from the walls, running down the smooth paint and flowing on to the floor. Only instead of forming puddles of liquid, it oozed between the floorboards and disappeared. Entire walls were covered with blood, blood that flowed freely like a mountain stream during the spring run-off. It had begun to run down the front door and Jon backed away, wiping the red goo from his hair.

"Jon! Don't move!! No...wait...move over to the window!! Move over to the window and stay there!!" The house was really trembling now, as well as the ground around it. Ron flew to the shed and began tossing items aside, searching.

"Come on...come on...I know you're here...." He carelessly threw things aside. A handsaw went flying, as did a toolbox and an old tin bucket.

"Come on...I know you're...there you are, you son of a gun." He grabbed the axe and yanked it out from a pile of odds and ends, grasping it near the heavy steel blade as he sprinted back across the yard and to the front door. He glanced over to the side and peered through the window to make sure that his son was out of the way, and swung.

The impact sent the blade through the door, splintering the wood around the wound. Ron turned and twisted the axe and pulled it free to swing again, but even as he did so the door began to repair itself. The next blow struck the same hole, tearing a bigger split in the strong, thick mahogany. He had difficulty removing the axe head this time, as the door began to fix itself around the heavy steel blade. Ron pulled with all his might and the door gave in, releasing the axe. He swung again, this time much harder, much more violently, and immediately withdrew the axe upon impact. He smashed the doorknob and it exploded in a dozen pieces, falling to the porch below. Instantly the metal fragments organized themselves and began leaping back in place but Ron swung the axe again, pulverizing the molding around the door.

"Hurry Dad!! Hurry!!" Jon was crying hard now with tears streaming down his cheeks, and he was holding the coffee can so tightly that he had kinked the side of it. Ron swung the axe relentlessly at the door, faster and harder. Every few seconds he looked back across the meadow through the downpour to see the pained look of shock and disbelief on Janet's face, her arms still tightly clutching Casey.

"Come on Dad!! Hurry!!" Jon choked. He was watching his father through the window, snapping his head around to survey the unbelievable scene unfolding about him. Blood had begun to drip over the windows, coating the glass in thick, runny crimson. Ron swung the axe harder and succeeded in tearing a hole in the bottom of the door. One more swing and the lower portion of the door gave way, sending wood splintering across the parlor inside the house.

Instantly Jon was at the door and the house began to shake violently. Already the tiny splinters of wood had begun to crawl back into place, edging back to the door.

"Duck down Jon!" Jon bent down and crawled beneath the broken door as a large piece of the wood flew back in place, pinning him to the floor.

"Help! Help me Dad!" he screamed, terrified. Ron picked up the axe again and carefully swung it towards the door.

"Keep down! Cover your face!" Jon did as he was told and his father swung harder, breaking away a portion of the

door, then another. Jon struggled and crawled forward from beneath the door. He was free.

The house rocked angrily back and forth, knocking both Ron and Jon to the porch. Instantly, the floorboards of the small patio began to writhe and bend, snapping and breaking, exposing a black, cavernous hole. Wood planks began to fall into the chasm and the entire porch began to give way as the house shuddered even more. Ron rolled off what was left of the porch and onto the grass and grabbed the hands of his son as he was being drawn down into the deepening crevice. Jon let go of the coffee can and it went tumbling below, bouncing off boards and falling into the depths of the widening abyss. The entire portion of the ground beneath the porch suddenly opened up like a giant cave, gaping wide and deep. Pieces of wood and shingles fell down the hole and disappeared, sucked into the black vortex beneath the lighthouse. The porch gave one final pull like an enormous gasp for air, using all of its strength. Jon dangled in space, suspended above the black aperture, held only by the tight grip of his father. The cavity was like a hungry mouth, the mouth of some awful animal, licking its lips and waiting to devour its next victim. Ron could feel the force of his son being pulled away, being pulled down into the dark hole. He held Jon's arms tightly and pulled with all his might.

"Hang on Jon!" he screamed over the deafening roar of destruction. *"Hang on Jon and don't let go!!"* Jon shot a panicked glance below him just in time to see one of his shoes pulled off and tumble away, vanishing into the deep fissure. Ron held his son firmly and pulled in a frenzy as

the hole continued its assault.

Too late, buddy boy.

Ron heard the voice in his head and gazed into the dark hole. The face of a man...of Virgil McClure...appeared again, reaching up out of the blackness, grasping at Jon's legs.

Like I said...a fair trade. What's fair is fair, doncha think, Ronnie?

Ron took a deep breath and pulled with all of his strength and might, tightening his grasp around Jon's wrists. Suddenly both he and Jon were flying, tumbling backwards, falling back and collapsing on to the wet grass. Ron continued to roll with his son until they were near the middle of the yard and away from the house. Without stopping he leapt to his feet and picked up Jon and ran with him, sprinting across the meadow through the driving rain.

The big oak tree wasn't providing much cover from the thundering storm, and both Janet and Casey were soaked to the skin. Janet was staring blankly up at the house and Ron turned, still holding Jon in his arms.

The house was a whirlwind of disaster. Shingles were flying madly off the roof, and the hardwood siding was splintering and falling away. The house indeed looked like it was breathing, inhaling deeply and exhaling heavily. Ron recalled the time years ago when he had watched *Wizard of Oz* for the first time, remembering the tornado that sent the house spiraling through the sky, along with people, animals, and that terrible woman on a bicycle. The scene before him indeed looked like something out of a science-fiction movie. Brilliant flashes of light emanated from within the lighthouse, illuminating the blood-stained windows. The whole building rattled and ripped at its very foundations.

"Come on!" Ron screamed above the noise. *"Let's get over to the other side of the island!"* They began to walk quickly across the open field as the rain beat down and the wind rushed against them. Lighting ripped through the clouds and blasts of thunder exploded like bombs in the dark sky.

Janet turned back around, as if she couldn't believe what was happening and had to have one more look just to be sure. Heavy raindrops pummeled her face and she squinted as the stinging water ran into her eyes. Her hair was flat and she wiped away a lock that had fell over her forehead, sticking to her cheek. Her eyes grew wide as she spoke.

"Ron...look." Ron stopped and turned. The yellow beacon atop the tower began to fade, gradually growing dim until it was completely out. The rain, once blown by the heavy wind, fell straight down in a heavy drizzle. The house had stopped shaking and looked suspiciously quiet in the ensuing storm. Shingles and wood planks littered the yard. Broken boards lay cast about, some a hundred feet or more from the building. The porch was completely gone, leaving a large gaping cavity under the front awning. The huge hole in the roof had returned and it appeared that the structure had shifted on its foundations, as there was a noticeable slant on the entire north portion. The house again looked like nothing more than an old, dilapidated farm building, abandoned and desolate, slowly falling apart.

"Come on," Ron said, and he began to turn and head

down the trail. Something caught his eye and he turned back again to look at the house.

A long, gray plank was slowly rising, standing on end. It paused in mid-air and suddenly shot towards the house, snapping into place. It was followed by another, and then another. Shingles began to arise from the ground after being tossed and scattered about. One by one they flew back to the roof, falling perfectly into place. Beams and supports sprang up and out of the black hole that just moments ago had enveloped the entire porch. It was like seeing an explosion on a movie screen, only backwards and in slow motion.

Ron and Janet stared in horror and bewilderment. The house was completely restoring itself and in minutes the entire lighthouse looked as if it were brand new, as if it were built that very day. And, as if it were the final crowning glory, the yellow beacon in the tower appeared in a flash, first very small, but growing quickly. It glowed like a harvest moon, brighter than Ron had ever seen, illuminating the lighthouse and the surrounding meadow.

Janet turned and began walking towards the trail, but Ron didn't follow. He stood in the heavy rain, looking up at the house, his terror turning to anger and indignation. He sat Jon down on the ground and immediately Janet grabbed his hand, pulling Jon close to her.

"Stay right here," Ron ordered. "Don't move."

"Where are you going?!?!" Janet asked incredulously. Ron didn't say a word as he ran through the grass and across the field.

◆ ◆ ◆ ◆

The shed was in shambles from having tore through the storage piles looking for the axe. Ron opened the door and kicked away a few old wood boxes and a couple plastic milk crates he had used to stash his tools in. He moved a few things aside and picked up two of the cans of oil that would be used to fuel the light in the tower. He carried them over to the summer kitchen and set them on the grass, returning for two more.

The house had been silent, but once again a low rumbling began from within. Ron could feel it beneath his feet as he picked up the can of oil and began pouring it over the side of the house. The house trembled angrily, but Ron kept pouring, emptying the first can and picking up the second.

A window exploded, and the glass went flying. Ron screamed and dropped the can of oil as jagged pieces of glass buried into his flesh. Relentless, he picked up the can and continued pouring and another window broke, only this time he protected his face and torso by raising the oil can and using it as a shield. The glass tore at his knuckles and the back of his hands and arms. He ran to the porch, picking up another can of oil in the process and began pouring the fluid over the wood patio. Oil spilled over his wounds and he winced in pain as the flammable liquid seeped into his cuts. Another window exploded and he dropped to the ground as the glass went sailing over him. He returned to his feet and he emptied the can, dashing back for the final five-gallon container. He finished off the entire can on the floor and the inside walls of the summer kitchen, throwing the empty, rusting drum down the hallway.

Ron reached into his pocket for the book of matches that he carried and his heart sank when he opened the cover. They were soaked. He dashed back to the shed, looking for something...*for anything....*

He quickly tossed various items aside, throwing them out of the shed, looking for something that could bring a spark. He banged a couple pieces of old pipe together, but nothing happened. He searched the shelves, sweeping their contents on to the floor and-

There. A blue and red box of Fire Chief kitchen matches sat innocently at the back of the top shelf. He reached for the box and shook it. Two matches tumbled within the small cardboard container. Ron slid the box open, then closed it quickly. He huddled over the box as he ran through the rain, stopping just before reaching the summer kitchen. The house was really shaking now, and Ron found it difficult to maintain his balance as the earth shifted violently beneath his feet. Every time he moved the lacerations caused him immense pain. Blood and oil covered his arms as well as his shirt and jeans. His clothes were shredded in places where the glass had ripped through.

He opened the box of matches and withdrew one of its two contents.

"Better make this good," he said to himself. He struck the match and it flared to life, but the head broke off and the tiny yellow ball blazed and spun wildly to the ground, extinguishing in the wet grass.

"Son of a bitch!" he complained aloud. There was only one match left. He huddled over the box and pulled out the final match.

"Come on, baby...this is all up to you." Carefully, he struck the match on the box. A spark flew off, but the match didn't ignite.

"Come on, come on...." The house began screaming at him through loud creaks and groans as it shifted and moved on its foundations. A large tremor nearly brought him to his knees, and he almost dropped the match. Again, he struck it against the box.

This time, the fire took. The sulphur exploded into a tiny yellow ball and Ron tossed it through the open door of the summer kitchen into a large pool of oil. The match tumbled to the floor, bounced a couple times, and lay in the puddle.

Nothing happened. The yellow flame grew smaller and faded, turning blue, just barely glowing.

"What the f-"

He no sooner had spoken the words when the porch suddenly erupted, sending flames across the floor and up the walls. The fire crept slowly at first as the oil ignited, then faster as the wood began to catch. A concussion of hot air blasted Ron and he covered his face as he jumped back, still in terrible pain from the glass cuts. He stepped back further.

The flames had quickly spread to the side of the house, and the oil ignited faster now. The summer kitchen was completely ablaze with flames licking through the screen and blanketing the ceiling, and the paint on the walls was bubbling and boiling in the intense heat.

Ron turned and began to run across the field, not stopping until he reached Janet and Casey and Jon. All three were watching the burning lighthouse that was now totally engulfed and roaring, even in the pouring rain. Flames leapt high into the sky and twisted in the wind, scorching the white brick conical tower. Loud groans and creaks drifted through the inferno, as if the house were screaming, screaming in pain, being burned alive. A truss gave way and part of the roof collapsed, sending a thick shower of amber sparks into the sky to be quickly extinguished by the rain. The light atop the conical tower shined strong, stronger than ever before, becoming a blinding ball of fire as intense as the sun. Suddenly the top of the tower exploded in an enormous fireball, sending up a black and orange mushroom cloud that seemed to envelop the entire island. Glass and metal could be heard falling through the trees, and Ron guided Janet's face away and pulled Jon and Casey close, protecting them from the falling debris.

"Come on!" Ron yelled over the storm and the roaring blaze. He put his arm around his son and motioned him along the trail, and Janet turned and did the same, carrying Casey in her arms. The wind continued to howl, thundering through the trees. Branches could be heard snapping and breaking all around them and a dead white pine succumbed

to the strain of the continuous wailing wind. It crashed through thick branches as it fell, not ten yards from the trail where the four were walking. Still wary of the possibility of encountering the dogs again, Ron picked up Jon in his arms and began to jog, and Janet did the same with Casey held tightly to her shoulder. The trail was muddied from the rain and large pools of water splashed as they continued though the thick swamp. They reached the edge of the forest and sprinted across the field, through the remains of the old village and to the water's edge. Pearson's boat was beached and a heavy line had been tied to a tree to keep it from drifting off.

"Thank God," Janet whispered.

"Tom!" Ron shouted. There was no answer. *"TOM!"* His eyes scanned the shoreline and the remains of the old village. Still not seeing the deputy, Ron waded into the water and looked in the boat. The key was in the ignition. Ron glanced up again, looking around the village.

He went to look for us, Ron thought, expecting to see the deputy at any minute. But he didn't appear.

He waded back and picked up Jon, carrying him to the boat and setting him inside. Janet was already in the water, and she climbed into the boat with Casey still wrapped around her neck.

"I'm going to go find him," Ron said.

"Wouldn't we have met him on the trail?" Janet asked.

"I don't know. There might be another trail. I'll run back and see if I can find him." He snapped open the glove compartment and shuffled a few papers around and finally pulled out a small leather case containing a .25 caliber semi-automatic. The gun was small, and he shoved the entire piece in his right front pocket.

"Stay here...in the boat. I'll be right back." Ron turned and sprinted back through the ruins of the town and over the field. Huge raindrops pelted his face and then it began to hail. White marbles hurled from the sky and Ron tried covering his head with his hands as he ran. The effort didn't do much good, and the stinging chunks drove at him as he ran faster towards the forest. Upon reaching the wooded trail the canopy of trees provided more shelter and Ron ran furiously along the path, splashing through puddles of water and ducking beneath low overhanging branches.

"*Tom!!*" He yelled as he ran. "*Tom!!*" It was getting darker, and within the hour it would be completely dark as night fell.

"*Tom!!*"

A light flickered through the branches.

"*Tom! Over here!*" Ron continued along the trail, catching a glimpse of the light as he grew closer.

A streak of lightning ripped open the sky and the roar of thunder blasted from above. Ron stopped.

It was *him*.

The man stood next to the towering cedar, holding a lantern and glaring back at Ron. The pickets around the grave had been strewn about, and a large pile of dirt grew from the base of the cedar. A shovel was planted in the ground.

Almost ready, the man spoke to Ron, his lips unmoving. *It's just about time.* He began to smile that same wicked, menacing smirk that Ron had seen back at the lighthouse.

He hung the lantern on a branch and slowly placed one hand on the shovel.

Ron flew into a rage.

"He's not coming back, Virgil! He's dead! He's been dead for along time and he's not coming back!!" The irony of his statement suddenly hit him. Here he was on an uninhabited island, yelling at someone who's been dead for fifty years, telling them that the dead don't come back.

Oh yes. Yes he is, Ron. He just needed a little help. McClure pointed at the hole in front of the cedar. Huge roots fingered over the hole, showing long scars and gashes from where they had been hit by the shovel. Ron stepped closer, peering into the pit.

They're wrong, Ron. And you're wrong. Everyone was wrong. Harmon is going to be back. Very soon now.

"No he's NOT Virgil!" Ron screamed above the boiling storm. *"I destroyed the lighthouse! It's gone and he's not coming back! Not tonight, not EVER!"* The wind and rain continued whirling about. Thunder and rain roared in his ears and Ron looked at the man who stood not ten feet from him. The skin on his face was pale and leathery. His eyes were sunk deeply into their sockets, and his cheekbones looked as if they were about to pierce through flesh. He was-

Lifeless? Ron heard in his head. *You think I'm lifeless? Wrong again, Ronnie. It is YOU who is lifeless. I am very much alive. Much more so than you have ever been, Ron. You want to see life? Go ahead. Take a look. You'll see.*

Ron inched closer, looking into the hole, holding one hand near his pocket that carried the .25 caliber. The roots of the cedar tree covered a large portion around the hole and Ron leaned from side to side, not wanting to get any closer, but he still couldn't see what Virgil was pointing to.

He took a step forward, peering into the unearthed grave.

The ground suddenly gave way under his weight and Ron fell, tumbling forward into the hole. His foot thumped on something hard and he wrapped his arms around a large root, holding with all of his strength. The sickly, dead corpse of Virgil McClure picked up the shovel and began pouring dirt back into the hole. Haunting, sickening laughter filled his ears drowned out the raging storm. Gritty brown mud hit Ron in the face and he closed his eyes as the wet dirt fell over him. He sputtered and spit, shaking his head, continuing to try and pull himself up. Another heap of dirt piled on him and he turned away, closing his eyes. Still another blast of mud came at him only this time he closed his eyes and swung one arm forward. It hit the shovel, and he grasped the metal blade with his hand. Mud dripped from his forehead and fell into his face and he kept his eyes closed, unable to wipe it away. He held fast to the shovel as Virgil tried to pull it out of Ron's grasp. Ron braced himself with the root and continued pulling, pulling harder and refusing to let go.

Come on, Ron thought. *Just a bit...a bit further....*

With one strong surge he pulled himself up enough to put one foot on a root. Ron pushed and rolled over the side of the hole, letting go of the shovel and rolling away. He continued rolling and then snapped to his feet, wiping the mud from his face and opening his eyes.

Virgil was gone.

Along with the pile of dirt, the hole, the shovel. The pickets were aligned as they had always been, worn and weathered from the years. The tall, thick grass around the cedar was unblemished. Only the old lantern remained, swinging gently from a branch. It grew dim, dwindling down and fading until it was just a tiny spark. Finally, it went out completely.

Ron turned and ran, thundering through the brush, not looking back.

Ron returned to the boat to find Janet huddled over Casey and Jon. She had found a large tarp and pulled it over them to shield them from the rain. The two children snuggled close together, each wearing bright white life vests. By now it had grown completely dark.

"You didn't find him?" she asked.

"Nowhere," he replied, wading into the water and leaping into the boat.

"But how can that be? He has to be here."

"We can't wait any longer. In a few minutes it's going to be too dark to make it back to the mainland. We'll leave and send someone back after him." The engine turned over and the boat idled. Ron jumped back out, ran to shore and untied the line, returning to the water to push the boat away from the beach. When the water was waist deep he climbed in, turned the boat around, and headed for the row of tiny lights on the mainland some two miles away. The waves on this side of the island weren't as severe as the ones pounding the southern shore near the lighthouse, but they were bad enough. The patrol boat was lifted and tossed about in the churning waters.

"Stay down in the bow!" he hollered. Janet and Casey and Jon huddled in the front of the boat beneath the tarp while the rain and wind sailed around them. Lightning flashed through the sky illuminating the Straits and the mainland. Ron could see the distant shore with every brilliant flash, and he tried to stay focused on a single light that blinked from the mainland coast. The boat rose up high on a swirling crest and the bow fell as the wave passed, slamming the fiberglass hull to the water. Jon and Casey screamed in fright but were unharmed. Ron tried to see the waves coming but it was impossible to know when each wave was about to slam into them. Often a flash of lightning would give him a glimpse of a roller closing in over them, but usually he had little or no warning before the waves swept over the boat. The white-capped swells loomed over him like mountains, plunging down angrily and pouring water into the boat. Ron remained diligent, keeping the boat aimed towards shore as the storm ripped at the tiny craft and its occupants. Janet held the children tightly in the front of the bow, holding them to her as she strained to brace herself for every onslaught of the tumultuous breakers.

Over the course of an hour, the lights Ron had focused on had grown closer. He could see the shoreline in the darkness now, and he could see the blue-green mercury vapor light constantly now. The raging storm refused to let up and showed no sign of passing soon. Six inches of water sloshed on the bottom of the boat but there was no way to bail it out.

Ron looked up through the mountains of waves ahead of the boat, focusing on the light. It appeared to be a yard light, a light on a telephone pole in someone's back yard. It remained as good of a target as any. Most people on the lake had some sort of small beach or swimming area, and he would have to try and reach one.

The boat lurched back as another huge wave thundered by. Ron gripped the wheel tightly, bracing himself as the boat rose on the swell and nose up. The wave passed, pitching the bow violently back to the water.

There was an ear-splitting explosion as the fiberglass shattered, ripping open the hull. Ron was thrust forward over the wheel and into the bow, tumbling over the tarp and into the water. The children were screaming and Janet was frantic. The boat had slammed into a rock just a few hundred feet from shore.

"Ron!?!?! Ron!?! Where-" Her voice was drowned out in the next wave as it into the boat, rolled lifting it back up and thrusting it forward. The tiny vessel lurched sideways, mortally wounded and filling with water. Janet and Jon and Casey spilled overboard into the lashing swells.

"Jon!! Casey!!" Janet screamed. Suddenly a white shape bobbed in front of her and she grasped at it, fumbling

madly in the frigid waters. It was Casey.

"Jon!! She shouted. "Jon?!?!? RON!?!?"

"Right here!" Ron yelled. *"I'm here!! I've got Jon!!"*

Oh thank God, Janet thought. Jon's white vest bobbed into view for a moment in the darkness. Jon and Ron were only a few feet away but it had been impossible to see or hear in the raging storm. Casey was crying and Janet was trying to console her daughter.

"Hold on tight, sweetie. Hold on tight."

"We have to swim to shore!" Ron shouted over the gale. *"Can you swim!?!?"* The question wasn't one of whether she could swim or not, as Janet had always been a good swimmer. The question was whether or not she could swim in conditions like this.

"I...I think so," Janet yelled back. She turned her attention to tiny Casey, shivering in her arms.

"Hold on around Mommy's neck," she instructed her. "Hold on *really* tight." Casey was still crying and she wrapped her arms around her mothers neck like a vise, holding on for life. Janet began to crawl through the rolling waves, and every few moments she caught a glimpse of Jon's white life vest.

"Ron!?!?" She called out every minute.

"Right here!" he shouted back, letting her know that he too was still there.

On a normal, calm day the swim to shore from where they were might have taken two minutes, but under the current conditions it was nearly impossible. Each swelling wave would lift the swimmers to the top of a roaring mountain, finally sending them to the depths of the valley to be assaulted by the next wall of water. It was like swimming up a hill, then digging out of a hole, up a hill, down a hole.

After nearly a half-hour in the unbearably cold waters, Ron finally reached the shore. He stumbled forward on a small rocky beach, carrying Jon in his arms. He set him down on the grass and returned to the water. Janet was still thirty feet from shore and Ron waded in for her, swimming back through the heaving waves that were slamming into the shore.

"Are you all right!?!?" He shouted as he reached her.

"Yes," Janet responded, sputtering and choking as a wave filled her mouth with water. Ron Pulled Casey from around her neck and the three finally made it to safety.

There were no words spoke as they left the water. Casey was sobbing in Janet's arms and Jon was sniveling as they walked through the yard and up towards the house. There were lights on inside, and as they approached Ron could see four figures, sitting at a table. They appeared to be laughing and playing cards.

They walked up the steps of a small wood porch and Ron rang the doorbell.

Sheriff Calhoun loomed over Ron, scribbling something

on a clipboard. In contrast to Pearson, Calhoun was a huge hulk of a man, well into three hundred pounds and standing nearly six and a half feet tall. His eyes were focused and unblinking as he spoke.

"Okay. So you burned the lighthouse and hiked to the harbor and found the boat. You say you didn't find Deputy Pearson. Then what?"

"I told you. We came back to the mainland. It was dark...I had no idea where the hell we could go, so we just found a piece of land and tried to beach the boat. That's when we must have hit the rocks or something. We swam to shore...then we went to the door of somebody's house, and they drove us here." Ron was getting tired of the Sheriff asking questions, the same ones over and over again. He lay back in the bed at Mackinac Straits Hospital in St. Ignace. He'd required a number of stitches to patch up his wounds, and the doctor had to remove over a dozen tiny pieces of glass that were tearing at his flesh every time he moved. Janet was sitting at his side, and Jon and Casey were sleeping on the only other bed in the sterile white room. He hadn't bothered to tell the Sheriff about the final incident at the grave, the hole, the shovel. There was a lot he didn't tell him. Maybe he would later. Maybe he wouldn't ever.

"Well I'm sorry you gotta go through this, Mr. Borders, but right now I've got a missing deputy and a patrol boat that is smashed to hell on the rocks. Pearson headed to the island to retrieve you and your family. You had his boat, but you claim you never saw him. Plus you were carrying Pearson's off-duty piece when you came to the hospital.

Now forgive me, but I gotta believe there's some sort of connection here."

"Well, I know he's on the island," Ron insisted. "He has to be. We just didn't see him. Our plan was to meet him at five and he was going to bring us back. But we never saw him."

The Sheriff drew in a deep breath and exhaled through his nose, creating a sound like a fast leak in a bicycle tire. The hiss faded as he exhaled through his nostrils. He stared intently at Ron.

"You want to tell me again just *why* you thought it necessary to set fire to the lighthouse...then attempt to come across two miles of water in conditions like this?"

The Sheriff wasn't able to get any new information from Ron or Janet. The whole thing was just crazy. Destroy the lighthouse? Why would Borders destroy the lighthouse and the tower? Calhoun didn't know what to think. Regardless, he had a bigger problem to worry about at the moment. He picked up the phone at the front desk of the hospital and dialed. It rang a few times before being answered.

"Coast Guard...2nd Class Petty Officer Mills speaking."

"Yeah...this is Sheriff Calhoun. We have kind of an

emergency here. I think we have a deputy stranded over on St. Helena Island...and we're gonna need to get him outta there tonight."

"Tonight? In this weather?"

The Sheriff briefly explained the situation to the commander.

"Well, I'll get it to the officer in charge, and we can try and send a boat over, Sheriff...but it'll be at least an hour before we can get there in these conditions."

"Do what you can. I'll get a few of the guys here together. I don't have any idea where we might find him, so be prepared to do some huntin'."

"Will do. At least we won't have any problem findin' the island tonight."

"What do you mean?"

"The light in the lighthouse. It's lit up pretty as can be."

Sheriff Calhoun paused nearly three full seconds before he spoke again.

"The tower light? In the lighthouse? Are you sure?"

"You bet," came the reply. *"You can see it for miles."*

EPILOGUE

June, 1999

The afternoon was nothing less than a beautiful, twenty-five cent picture-perfect postcard. Sunny and warm, not a single cloud to mar the rich blue sky. Tourists were busy ferrying to Mackinac Island, the span of the great Mackinac Bridge was filled with weekend travelers heading north and south, and dozens of boats and colorful sailboats dotted the Straits. A helicopter flew high over the water, its two occupants gazing down at the crystal blue waters.

"There she is," the pilot said loudly over the drone of

the engine. "Take a look over there." He pointed down and began to swing the chopper around for a closer look. Below, the St. Helena Island lighthouse came into view through the towering trees.

"Unbelievable," the passenger said, shaking his head.

"Built in 1873. Lot of history there."

The helicopter circled the area once before landing gently in the field adjacent to the old building. The two men got out, looking across the meadow at the old, run down lighthouse. Dragonflies dived and flitted over the field and the air was filled with the steady, monotone buzz of locusts. The two men started across the meadow and stopped beneath the conical tower.

"What do you think?" the pilot asked.

"Lots of work to be done. *Lots* of work. But...yeah. I like it." The old lighthouse was falling apart, with shingles missing from the roof and wood siding slowly rotting away. Debris littered the area, and the structure seemed to be caving in on itself. The porch roof sunk down, bending under years of strain as the timbers slowly began to grow weary with age.

"We've been trying to get this restored for years. At least ever since I became chairman of the International Lighthouse Preservation Society back in 1961."

"Been at it a while, huh?" the passenger asked, chuckling.

"Well, a *little* while. I retired from law practice in '85. Now lots of lighthouses keep me pretty busy. That's why it's nice to have this 'copter to buzz around in. Lots of lighthouses on the Great Lakes. But this one-" He pointed across the field at the old home and the graying conical tower- *"This* one is my favorite."

"I read in the paper about some guy last summer who was supposed to restore this place. Some...." The man paused, trying to remember the man's name.

"Borders," the chairman finished. "Ron Borders. A shame. I don't know what happened. Went nuts or something. Talked about some pack of wild dogs that he claims roamed the island. Left with his family in the middle of a storm sayin' that he'd burned the lighthouse to the ground, saying it was haunted. You know. Crazy stuff. Coast Guard went over this entire island for over two weeks...never found so much as a dog track. In fact myself and a few others in the ILPS went over this island with a fine-toothed comb. We didn't find a thing. "

The passenger continued to survey the lighthouse, his gaze shifting from the tower and back to the old building.

"Doesn't look so burned down to me," he offered.

"Nor anybody else, either. But apparently there had been some recent deaths in Borders' family. Probably just the pressure of everything got to him and he cracked up."

"What about that deputy that disappeared?"

"Drowned, they presume. Nobody had any business being on the water in those conditions, especially in a small boat like that. Not even a sheriff's deputy. It really was tragic. They never found him. 'Course, with the currents in the Straits, he could be carried to Lake Erie by now."

A few seconds went by before the two men slowly began to walk through the grass towards the lighthouse.

"Windows are in good shape," the passenger said.

"Yeah, go figure," the chairman replied. "Those are about the only things that don't need any work."

The two men stopped, looking up at the old structure. The old chairman turned, smiling.

"Well Carl...what do you think?"

"I think it's great. I'm not sure what my wife is going to think, and of course I'll have to check with her before I give you an answer. But I'm sure she'll be more than up for it. This'll be a dream come true."

"You folks have any kids?"

"Yeah. Three of'em. Eight, ten, and twelve. All boys." He laughed as he spoke, then paused. "Will...will that be a problem, Mr. McClure?"

"No," the old pilot said, shaking his head. "No problem at all. And can the 'Mr. McClure' crap. It's Harmon. *But you can call me Harry, just like everybody else.*"

THE END